£9.99.

CW00495013

Growing Up in Sowerby

… and more

Jean Illingworth

Best wishes.
Jean Illingworth

RP

Published by Royd House
The Book Case
29 Market Street
Hebden Bridge
West Yorks.
HX7 6EU
www.bookcase.co.uk

© Jean Illingworth, 2008

Front cover photograph: the author Jean Smith with friend Terry Dixon, c. 1947

Back cover photographs:
the author, © Halifax Evening Courier,
and in 1953

We have made all reasonable efforts to ensure that the reproduction of all content on these pages is done with the consent of copyright owners and any errors or omissions are unintentional.

ISBN: 978-0-9556204-7-8

Foreword

As an "off comer" of 30-plus years from Essex (yes, I did possess a pair of white stilettos) I came to live in Calderdale in 1976 after marrying my husband Glyn, a local who grew up in Sowerby.

I was enthralled by the beauty of the area, especially from the hilltops, and thought, "This really is 'God's own county'," in comparison to the flatness of Essex, and set out to explore it.

I first became aware of Jean through her contributions to the local paper with her articles on life as a child in Sowerby village.

As a keen walker, I have led walks through the village entitled "Historical Sowerby" for the Ramblers and other groups, including the Calderdale Festival of Walks, and have asked Jean to accompany us to tell us all about the village, including the history, the wonderful old buildings and the characters who lived there.

A large part of Sowerby village has disappeared, but thanks to Jean's stories and memories, it is possible to picture the village as it was. Many fine buildings remain including St. Peter's Church, a Georgian gem on our doorstep and a fine focal point, which can be seen for miles.

To me, the village of Sowerby is very special, with panoramic views across Midgley Moor, Crow Hill, Ovenden Wind Farm, the Luddenden valley, Emley, and Norland moor, and much more on a clear day.

Jean has a clear love and passion of Sowerby, the area where she grew up, which is evident from her lively infectious interest: she brings to life the characters with her stories.

Anyone who knows the village will have their childhood memories rekindled with a nostalgic look back to a bygone age where the reader is transported back in time.

Jean feels it is important that these memories of life then are written down before they are lost forever.

This book will be a valuable reference to Sowerby in years to come.

Former Councillor Judy Gannon

Sowerby from the church tower, post World War II.

Preface

This is the beginning of my childhood memories, recorded on my new computer, starting on March 30, 2005. Having retired from my part-time job with Tesco in Market Street, Halifax last May, I attended Sowerby Bridge library to learn computer skills. At the age of 60, the idea was rather daunting but entirely necessary for recording my memories to produce this book.

My previous booklet had been hand-written, and friends helped me with the computer side, so I knew I had to acquire some knowledge of the machine. My skills are very basic, but hopefully I shall succeed with my aim of recording my childhood in Sowerby and some historical background of the village. I have also spoken to other people who have their own memories of Sowerby, which they have kindly related to me.

Acknowledgements

Thanks to Heather Karpiki and her staff at Sowerby Bridge Library, for their help and support when I attended a Learn Direct Course on how to use a computer, persuading me to continue when I felt like giving up and encouraging me to work towards my goal of writing a book about my childhood in Sowerby.

Thanks to John Furbisher, Editor of the *Evening Courier,* for allowing me to reproduce the "Sowerby Ghost Story" and to reproduce three photographs.

Sincere thanks to my friends Pat Dixon and Muriel Maskill for their informative pages of written memories.

Thanks to all the people who have talked to me, either in their homes, in my home, by telephone or letter, on the bus or in the street. They shared their stories with me - I hope they enjoyed relating them to me, as much as I relished listening to them.

Thanks to my friend Maggie Woods for her proof reading and giving my writing a format.

My thanks to Judy Gannon for writing the Foreword for my book.

Special thanks to Felicity Potter and Kate Claughan of The Book Case, Hebden Bridge, Felicity for her editing skills and Kate for her photographic knowledge.

For all their advice, help and support throughout in the production of my book, I am extremely grateful.

Contents

Many thanks to the people who loaned or allowed me to copy their photographs:

Mary Chapman (Haigh)
Mary Dale
Muriel Dewhirst (Wilson)
Lesley Ellison (Wilcock)
Marion Elwin (Hitchen)
Malan Ford
Marion Greenwood
Ken Harrison
Roger and John Heap
Margaret Jowett
Sheila Jowett
John Kerridge
Margaret Kerridge
David Kershaw
Muriel Maskill
Kathleen Meadowcroft (Lum)
Rev Jane Powell
Blanche Riley-Gledhill
Joyce Wright (King)
Sowerby Bridge Library

Origins and Changes

Sowerby village was a very special place in the 1940s and '50s. Everyone knew everyone else and social life revolved around the two pubs – the Church Stile and the Star Inn, the three chapels – Providence Methodist, Rooley Lane Methodist and Old Green Congregational Chapel at the top of the village; also St Peter's Church, the cricket field down Back Lane and the bowling green and tennis courts above.

Mentioned in the Doomsday Book of 1085-6, "Sorebi" means a farmstead on sour ground with "sour" meaning muddy. Up to 1274, manorial courts were held at Sowerby, but from that time were transferred to Wakefield. In 1332 the manor again reverted to the Crown. The name Seur Bye is also mentioned in the Doomsday Book as one of the nine Berewics within the Manor of Wakefield. The Saxon name meant "safe habitation". There were further references to cattle rearing and sheep pasture in the 14th-century manorial records. It was an important part of the Manor of Wakefield and in the early Middle Ages was in the hands of the Warrenne family, Earls of Surrey.

Town Gate, meaning "Main Street", runs through the village and is about 250 yards long.

Town Gate, from the church tower, 1960s.

There may have been a hunting lodge, as the hunting of deer and wild boar was recorded. There was also perhaps a castle in Sowerby – Mr Sam Fox, for many years our neighbour at The Curatage in Pinfold Lane, told me that it was probably a wooden fortification, which would command extensive views across the valley. Several excavations have taken place in the fields to the rear of Castle Hill (built in 1662) but nothing was ever found. It was also rumoured that there was an underground tunnel or passageway running from Castle Hill towards the bottom of Rooley Lane. This may have been discovered when demolition work was taking place opposite Castle Hill where there was a building known as Ing Farm, comprising a house and a stable. One of the workmen discovered stone steps from the centre of the house which led to the entrance of what was thought to be an old tunnel running under the road and linking up with the property at Castle Hill. It is recorded that a Mr Arthur Bradley of 7, Dob, found a George III (1683-1760) coin on the site.

In 1929 Sowerby New Road was completed and during the '30s, council or corporation housing was built. The Beechwood estate engulfed acres of fields that separated the village of Sowerby from Sowerby Bridge and turned it into a built-up area. The houses were needed to accommodate people who had been living in slum conditions, particularly those from the West End area of Sowerby Bridge or Bogden as it was sometimes called. After the Second World War, Sowerby Bridge Urban District Council began to redevelop the centre of Sowerby and build a council estate between Rooley Lane and Dean Lane. In December 1959, the 1,000th council house was completed at 65, Rooley Heights. One side of Town Gate was demolished, robbing the village of some of its most historic and interesting buildings, including the Rawson Almshouses (where a row of shops now stands). Almshouses had stood in Town Gate since the early eighteenth century when Elkanah Horton of Thornton provided in his will for the building of six houses. They were rebuilt by the late John Rawson in 1861, and then later demolished in the 1950s when a sum of £3,000 was needed for repairs to the properties. With an annual income of £16 and 5 shillings, the charity could not afford to continue the struggle. When the private water supply threatened to run out, and with no indoor sanitation, the houses were pulled down.

Opposite stands Sowerby Hall built by Elkanah's father Joshua. It is believed to be the earliest existing building in the village, dating from 1646, and features mullioned windows and stonework tracery. The rear of the house faces the main road and the carved heads above a window at the side of the hall in King Street are not seen often, unless one is aware of their presence. These are thought to have been removed from one of the earlier St Peter's Churches and incorporated in the building. Providence Chapel (where the three town houses are) was built by stalwart adherents to the Temperance movement in 1876. They were unable to conduct their Band of Hope in the Wesleyan Chapel in Rooley Lane and broke away to form a new congregation. The last service was held on the 26th August 1961, the building was demolished in about 1964-5 and three town houses built on the land. Next in the street stood Nos. 31- 45 Town Gate, a row of houses with an archway through the middle of them. Some were through houses, some back-to-back. Haigh's farm above and opposite was later called Haigh's Buildings and contained dwellings Nos. 47-51. When demolition started, it was discovered by Frank Atkinson of Halifax Museums Service that within the 17th-century stonework there was the timber frame of a 14th-century hall.

Haigh's Buildings, c. 1950.

Originally one building, it was known as "Rich Man's Dwelling". It was dismantled and presented to Durham County Council to be rebuilt on a 15-acre site which would become Barnard Castle's new Folk Museum. Later this was to be Beamish Museum which opened in 1971. Beams were numbered to be re-assembled and taken by road to Durham. There was also talk of some of the building being shipped to America, but none of this happened, at either destination, and this piece of local history sadly faded away.

Haigh's Buildings during demolition.

The charming 17th-century Sowerby Post Office with the stone porch opened for that purpose in 1914 and remained there until 1960 when it was transferred lower down Town Gate to the parade of new shops, built where the Almshouses had stood. The forge and smithy next to the Post Office were also demolished. Two houses opposite The Royd were also demolished, Nos. 57 and 59 Town Gate, where there had been reports of some "ghostly happenings" during the 1950s. So the left hand side of Town Gate (looking up the street from St Peter's Church) was destroyed as the building programme began. If the buildings had remained the village of Sowerby could have been a bigger tourist attraction than Heptonstall. Opposite the forge the old radio relay house remains, No. 38, now called Apple Cross Cottage. Here people used to take their wireless accumulators to be re-charged. In earlier days it was a barber's shop. The Royd still remains but the appearance has changed with modernisation – it is now flat-fronted and the old character of the building has been lost. There was an attempt at "improvement" to The Royd in the 1970s but this stripped the property of many original features and the building was spoilt. The next alterations were in 1992 and there was another project to restore some of the lost features with mullion windows replaced and internal beams restored or replaced. The house numbers there were 40, 42, 44 and 46. Castle Hill looks the same externally but the house where Mr and Mrs Joe Morgan lived has been incorporated into what was Mr Standeven's cobbler's shop, also a tiny dwelling at the rear, lived in at one time by a man called Theodore Speake, and is now appropriately called Trinity Cottage. The Spinks and the Nicholls lived at Castle Hill. The fish and chip shop was below Providence Chapel and was owned during my childhood by Jack Wilcock. He also had a hen pen situated in between No. 36 Highfield Place and the radio relay house. Two recently-built detached houses now stand there but this side of the street is also changing and a detached house is to be built where a garage stood at the side of the semi-detached house opposite the bottom of Rooley Lane; Kathleen Jowett lived here when I was a girl. Other planning applications have also been submitted to convert the building that was Alec Smith's joiners' workshop – now a printer's – into two apartments (plan later refused). So even what we had left is changing, not always for the better as we seem to end up with a mish-mash of designs and types of property, which in reality do not fit in or complement their surroundings. The three link-detached houses built on the former graveyard at Rooley Lane are a prime example: they have been built several years, but remain unsold. Hazel Parkin still lives in a cottage at Wesley Place; the area is set back in between where the chapel and Sunday School buildings stood. Her father George was caretaker there. The owners of The Manse at Well Head have purchased the graveyard of Old Green Chapel, to prevent any building from taking place on the land. Along Dob Lane opposite Chapel Terrace, land in the corner of the field was on the market during May 2003 for a large detached family home to be built.

Church Stile Farm was advertised for sale in May 2001 with planning permission for three individually designed detached residences to be built. The buildings for conversion were the large barn and mistal, the single-storey stable / bull hole, and also a single-storey animal holding outbuilding. Offers of around £225,000 were invited.

Changes are also to take place up at Town Farm: planning permission has been granted to convert the barn into a dwelling and five detached residences to be built on land to the west of the farm.

Coming into the world

I was born at 32, Town Gate, Sowerby.

My entry into the world was a little premature. About three weeks before I was due to arrive, my mother thought she was going into labour on the night of May 27th 1944. A phone call was made to our family GP, Dr Harold W. Morck in Sowerby Bridge, to explain the situation. He replied: "It's indigestion, woman, go back to bed." A few hours later I was born downstairs in front of the fire onto a white towel. Perhaps the doctor did attend after I was born; I am not sure about this. Maybe there was a visit from Nurse Kleindienst, an Austrian lady who was the district nurse and lived in Sowerby New Road. In later years I remember seeing her dressed in her navy gabardine coat and bowler-type hat and carrying her medical bag. Or perhaps Nurse Margaret Farrell, who was a family friend, had come up to our house that night from her home in the middle of Sowerby Hall, lower down Town Gate. The date was May 28th and it was also the Sunday School anniversary at Old Green Chapel, a place I would attend throughout my childhood.

Dad & Mum, date and resort unknown, probably mid-1930s.

My mother was called Emma Jane Smith (her maiden name as well as her married name). She was born on January 16th 1913 at Boothwood, Rishworth. Her father was called Irvine Smith and her mother Daisie Smith, formerly Willoughby. According to the marriage certificate of September 24th 1935 at Halifax register Office, he was a journeyman-papermaker. My father Arthur Smith was 28 years old and mother 22 years old when they married. He was described as a motor coach driver – this was for Ripponden and District who ran coaches before delivering freight. He was living at "Spring Avon", Ripponden, Barkisland, where he was lodging there with his friend Trevor Dixon and family; his father's name was Isaac Smith, a farmer.

My brother David and myself walking on the pier at Llandudno, late 1940s.

When I was six and my brother David thirteen years old, our father left my mother for another woman. This led to mother having a struggle to bring David and myself up during the following years. My parents were legally separated for more than twenty years and then finally divorced.

Opposite where I now live in Pinfold Lane is Wood Lane: this is to the rear of a row of terraced houses called Pinfold Green. Our friends Marion Greenwood and her daughter Susan live at Littlewood Lane Barn and Littlewood Lane Farm, respectively. A little lower down the lane to the right, a narrow lane leads to Wood Lane Hall, a yeoman's residence built by John Dearden in the reign of King Charles I, now Grade One listed and described as one of Sowerby's finest 17th-century buildings.

Wood Lane Hall in the 1980s.

It was originally a timber structure and encased in stone in 1649. The central feature of the building is a two-storey porch with Doric columns and a rose window above, similar to the one at Kershaw House. The Sugden family lived here for many years. As a child and later when I started to work in Halifax, I remember travelling on the upper deck of the bus and, as Christmas time approached, seeing the tall illuminated Christmas tree that was erected at the front of the hall.

The hall came onto the market when the last surviving sister Miss Margery Sugden died, and was offered for sale by public auction on February 8th 1995 by Brearley-Greens of Halifax. The hall was open for viewing on two Saturday mornings before the auction and the number of people who turned up was quite staggering. Pinfold Lane and the other access road from Sowerby New Road, via Daisy Lea, were full of vehicles belonging to curious would-be purchasers who came to view this interesting building. One of its unusual features was bedroom No. Six, "The Ship's Cabin", so-called apparently because a previous Sugden owner had enjoyed cargo ship cruising, and this bedroom had been turned into a ship's cabin which contained cruising memorabilia, even a life jacket! I ventured down to look at this house I had known all my life but never seen the interior. It was impressive but one doesn't get the true "picture" when the property is more or less empty. The kitchen sticks in my mind, with a lot of the utensils still there. I have never seen such a large frying pan in my life: it must have been capable of frying many eggs at one time. The purchasers of the Hall were a local family.

The village's main street had cobbles before the laying of Tarmac in later years and the street lighting was by gas lamps. There were churches and chapels in the village and all were well supported and attended, with good congregations and several generations of families supporting them.

St Peter's Anglican Church, at the bottom of Town Gate, is built in the classical style of the eighteenth century and is one of the finest Georgian churches outside London. It was built by Halifax stonemason John Wilson who copied the design of Holy Trinity Church in Leeds. It opened for worship on the January 3rd 1763 and the tower was added in 1781. The external walls are pilastered and topped by ornamental balustrades in contrast to the more orthodox pinnacles to the tower. Inside the church the statue of John Tillotson greets you. He was born in the seventeenth century at nearby Old Haugh End and went on to become the Archbishop of Canterbury. He was a man of liberal views and had great tolerance. He married one of Cromwell's nieces, he gave to the poor but died penniless, and he was a greatly loved man of the people.

The church has beautiful rococo plasterwork created by Giuseppe Cortese, an Italian who spent most of his life in Yorkshire decorating public buildings and country houses. The great roof columns are cut in half by the massive galleries. The chancel has a colonnaded east window and large panels with relief figures of Our Lord and Moses, rich plasterwork in medallions and a coat of arms. The chancel arch is supported by columns with gilt classical capitals and the whole effect of this rich chancel with its plaster carving and wood panelling is quite stunning.

St Peter's Church, c. 1906.

The eight bells in the bell tower were made by John Taylor and Co. at their foundry in Whitechapel in London. They were a complete ring of eight and were cast in 1781. The bells were removed and re-cast in 1954 at their Loughborough foundry. The recasting was done to commemorate the Coronation of Queen Elizabeth II on June 2, 1952. Four of the bells were donated by the Stansfeld family, who, along with the Rawson family, had connections with the church for generations and contributed to St Peter's throughout its existence.

The bells before restoration.

Bell ringers at St Peter's Church: left to right, Brian Wilson, Donald Hoyle, Harry Robinson, Harry Lumb, Stuart Hawksworth, Cedric Clarke kneeling.

Bell ringers in the ringing room.
Left to right, Rear, Stuart Hawksworth, Kenneth Harrison, Cyril Sutcliffe.
Front, Harry Lumb, George Briggs, Thomas Brown, Donald Hoyle, Edgar Wilde.

One of the new bells being tuned at the foundry in Loughborough.

Long-serving bellringer Tommy Brown with the re-cast bells. Saint Peter's Infant school, rear left, and St Peter's Square with archway.

To celebrate 240 years at St Peter's Church, over the weekend of Saturday September 30th 2006 and Sunday 1st October, a programme of events was held. The celebrations were a success and more than £500 was raised: the church was open for visitors and access to the belfry and to see the bells was allowed – visitors could even have a try at bell-ringing. John Kerridge presented a local history slide show across the road in the Community Centre. It was fascinating to see his excellent collection of slides of Sowerby throughout the years, and see what changes have taken place. Sadly, an act of vandalism has recently put more strain on the fund-raising of the parish. Bricks have been thrown though the magnificent stained glass east window causing damage that will cost thousands of pounds to repair and to protect the window in future. There is also damage to one of the side upper square windows facing St Peter's Avenue.

Bells up in position "ready to ring the changes".

19

St Peter's Infants School, opposite the Church, is now a private nursery for children. Further up the main road on the right-hand side (where three town houses now stand) was **Providence Methodist Chapel**, a large building with gardens at each side of the front entrance. To the rear there were fields, later to be built on, with the coming of council house development.

Providence Methodist Chapel, pre-war.

Rooley Lane Chapel, Sowerby.

Next were **Rooley Lane Methodist Chapel and Sunday School**, just above and opposite what used to be the Grammar School, which opened on October 4th 1875 and closed at Christmas 1904.The school was then divided into dwellings. The original Old

Wesleyan Chapel was built in 1787, and later destroyed by a fire in March 1876. The replacement new Methodist Chapel and Sunday School were built and opened in 1877. Lessons continued to be taught at the Grammar School (Bairstow's Endowed School) opposite until the buildings were complete.

Sowerby Congregational Chapel (known as "Old Green"), early 20th century.

At the junction of Dob Lane and Well Head stood the **imposing "Old Green" Congregational Chapel**. The Gothic-style chapel with spire was built in 1861 at a cost of £2,300 and designed by the architect Mr John Hogg. Later it was called Sowerby United Reformed Church.

Continuing along Dob Lane and Higham, passing The Manse on the right, to the top of the hill (where the Steep Lane bus terminus used to be), then uphill to the left, on the right stood **Steep Lane Baptist Chapel** and Sunday School. On April 30th 1986 the roof on Steep Lane Chapel was declared unsafe and on February 25th 1987 it was agreed to reduce the building to a single story. The opening and dedication services were held on May 13th and 14th, 1989.

Steep Lane chapel at its original size.

Steep Lane Chapel at its reduced size.

Down Back Lane and Saint Peter's Avenue, passing White Windows on the left (now a Cheshire Home) heading towards Sowerby Bridge: at Quarry Hill were St George's Church and also a school, which merged with Sowerby New Road Infants in 1959. This school opened for pupils on October 8th 1900 and celebrated its centenary in

October 2000. Several years ago St George's School was converted into housing and the church more recently into apartments.

Also in the area was the **United Methodist Church at Boulderclough** (known as Clough "Oile Chapel"); it was built by the community in 1882 as a flat-fronted building. The ground and the building of the church cost £900. Later in 1885 members of the church decided on a new building, but it took fourteen years to raise most of the £3,000 needed, through holding church concerts, sales of work and other efforts. Items from the church interior were stored down at Whitworth's mill at Swamp by the dam. Meetings and services were also held there.

The new building was in the style of the French Renaissance and the two conical towers were added, these flanking a portico with four arches. Inside was a semi-circular arrangement of pews. Figures taken from the *Centenary Souvenir Book 1822-1922* list:

Total baptisms	537
Marriages (since 1901)	47
Interments	546
(as per records able to trace)	

Boulderclough Church in 1945.

The first marriage to be held there took place on March 9 1907, when Mr Willie Pickles, second son of Mr and Mrs Jont. Pickles of Highfield Place, Sowerby and Miss Edna Mitchell of Finkle Street were married. Both the bride and groom were connected with the Sunday school and the church, which eventually closed in September 1979. The church was then sold and has since undergone extensive alterations to be converted to living accommodation. Near the church there was a row of four cottages, now demolished, and a general store selling a variety of goods. One of the cottages was a home for the church caretaker to live in. The last caretaker was Mr Ernest Crabtree who lived at 17, Clough Buildings, Boulderclough. He died aged 83 in May 1985 and he had been the caretaker for about fifteen years until the church closed down. He had also worked as a weaver at the former Fairlea Mills at Luddenden Foot for twenty years and as a farmhand and gardener at Wood Lane Hall for fourteen years. His son Trevor lived in the USA. Below in the clough across a bridge were eleven homes and a Working Men's Club. These were flooded out after a cloudburst in about 1953. Two new houses were built there. The stream flowing down the clough used to serve Swamp Mill owned by Robert Whitworth and Co, further down the valley.

The Hen-Pecked Club held their meetings at Boulderclough Church. This organisation, or the International Order of the Hen-pecked Clubs as it was also known, was founded in 1904 by six Methodist preachers who met in an uninhabited cottage in Cragg Vale. An all-male club, it ceased about 30 years ago. Their venues were secret and some members travelled distances to attend. The annual meeting took place on Easter Monday, and was not "a boozy affair". New members had to be married men on initiation, the whole joke of the Order being that if a man were really hen-pecked he would not be allowed to join the club in the first place!

My friendship with Joyce Wright (née King), one of the "characters" of Boulderclough, began after our return to Sowerby from King Cross in 1973 (we had lived there after our marriage in 1969). I knew of her but we had never met until I became an "Avon lady" and she was one of my regular customers. She has always been very interested in the history of this area and also has many stories to relate about her life and experiences. She was born at Bullace Trees in Triangle in July 1937 and her father William King, who came from Long Cliff in Settle, has been described by Joyce as a "rough diamond". Her mother Annie Mitchell was born at Rawson Farm, Mill Bank. She had an older brother and when Joyce was six months old, they moved to Acre Farm in Boulderclough. They rented the property, which had once been a fish and chip shop, from Matty Clough and here they had a smallholding, keeping mostly hens, ducks and geese. These all had to be destroyed and sheds burnt when fowl pest broke out in 1938.

Her father used to deliver milk for Crabtree's of Brockwell to people living in the Beechwood estates. Later when he had some cows, Joyce and her friend Pat Priestley would pull and push a bogie with two milk churns full of milk all the way along Pinfold Lane up to the Church Stile pub! This would not be an easy task to do as the final stretch is steep! The bogie and churns were then left outside the pub for collection by Peter Moore's father to supplement his own milk supply. After school the bogie was picked up again by the girls and an easier journey made back home. Her brother would sometimes give a lift home on his bicycle to pals, when school finished: this meant one person on the crossbar, one on the handlebars, and another one behind him! Possible in those days of little traffic, but still quite a balancing feat!

William King delivering milk in Beechwood, 1930s.

Haymaking at Boulderclough.

Leslie Stead, 1950s.

A "glamour pose" from Joyce King, haymaking,
in the Chapel Field, Boulderclough, 1953.

Joyce's dad made a sledge for her and wanted to test it himself before she used it so he set off down the fields where they lived. It went so well that he couldn't stop and continued through several fields below before he came to a halt. He also worked as a handyman for the Rawson's at Brockwell and rode his bicycle to get there from Boulderclough. When Joyce was six years old she attended Fenella Rawson's wedding in 1943 to an Argentinean man called Wolf Watkins at St Peter's Church, and saw the bride arriving in a pony and trap. One day her father was driving his horse and flat cart along Pinfold Lane and when he reached Row Lane Bottom, a lorry belonging to Riley's at Jack Hey Farm coming in the opposite direction caught the cart. Mr Wright, the horse and the cart crashed through the wall and into the field next to the lane. Luckily there were no serious injuries. Mr Wright was a gravedigger at Steep Lane Chapel and at Boulderclough Church. There was a problem at Steep Lane as the ground there would sometimes become water-logged and the prepared graves would occasionally fill up with water! When the graves were removed from West End Chapel in Sowerby Bridge, he assisted in the removal of the remains. Bones were collected and placed into smaller containers while a policeman stood on duty. Some bodies would have been buried wearing items of jewellery and these were removed and tagged with names where possible, to be returned to any surviving relatives.

As a fourteen-year-old, Joyce had had a fall from a wall which was to have serious consequences. Years later she began to feel ill and it was diagnosed that one of her kidneys was damaged, had shrivelled and died. She was admitted to McCrea ward at the Royal Infirmary in Halifax in 1967 when she was 30 and her daughter Yvonne was ten years old. Her stay lasted for two months as before an operation could take place she had to be given blood as she was anaemic. The damaged kidney was removed, a rib also and the appendix taken out. One of the patients was put off the soup she had ordered the next day when it turned out that the variety was kidney! She didn't eat it, needless to say. Within four months Joyce was back doing full time work. In 1986 when she was 49 she began to feel very tired and most jobs became "an effort". Tests confirmed that her other kidney was also failing. So three times a week she travelled to St James Hospital in Leeds for dialysis treatment which took four hours at a time. With the help of her husband Colin and Yvonne, as well as her good friends and neighbours, Joyce managed to cope with a now restricted diet. This treatment continued for nine months, and Joyce was now on the transplant waiting list. Three days before Christmas she had a telephone call to say a kidney was available, but this turned out to be a false alarm. Then in February 1987 a donor kidney was available for a successful transplant operation. Since her recovery Joyce has been a supporter and fundraiser for the St James Patients' Association. When the chapel closed at Boulderclough, Joyce and a group of friends decided to meet together once a month. Calling themselves "The Tuesday Night Girls", they have raised £16,000 pounds for the charity, donated bric-a-brac has been collected and sold on stalls on Sowerby Bridge market, raffle tickets sold and many fundraising events held.

When Joyce married Colin Wright in 1956, they lived in Providence Place at Sowerby New Road, moving after a few months to 84, Wakefield Road, Sowerby Bridge. When their daughter Yvonne was three years old, Joyce's dad had to go into hospital for a hernia operation. While he was incapacitated she would come up to the farm on the 7.30 am bus with Yvonne in tow, and see to the feeding and upkeep of the animals. This continued until his full recovery. Joyce has always worked; one of her jobs was cleaning for farmer Kenneth Hitchen and his wife Elsie at Ing Head Farm, Luddendenfoot. This was usually on Monday and Friday afternoons. Kenneth then decided that Joyce could be put to better use helping him, leading to a five-day week bottling milk and swilling the mistals out. This led to a weekly routine of helping Kenneth to deliver milk. Her hours working at the farm would be flexible depending on demand and the season of the year. Sometimes, if she slept in, Kenneth would knock on the door to get her up and out of bed. More than once she has hurriedly thrown a coat over her nightdress and delivered the locals their pinta in this unusual attire! One of the perks of the job was to have free milk for twenty-four years.

Joyce also worked for some time as a cleaner for Saville Rowntree at Stye's Farm.

Leslie Stead, haymaking during the '50s.

Pubs and shops

There were two bakeries in Shield Hall Lane – Broadbent's a little way up, and nearer the top was Lumb's bakery – they used to do two local deliveries a week. The building and outbuildings are now converted into housing. Harris Broadbent and his brother Etson ran the bakery at Shield Hall. Harris had four children, Barrie, Rodney, Margaret and Graham. Rodney was at school with me and was nicknamed Yo-Yo, pronounced "yoi-yoi"! The bakery made bread and tea-cakes, buns and cakes and Cornish pasties. Joyce King worked for Broadbent's and used to fill the trays with baking and then load up the vans for delivery to local shops and people around the area. They did three deliveries a week on Mondays, Thursdays and Saturdays. When she worked on a Saturday morning with Rodney, Graham and David Sutton, there was a lighter atmosphere and some horse-play would take place! On one occasion Joyce was put into the huge mixer – fortunately the blade had been removed!

The King's Arms at Boulderclough was the scene of a tragedy on the night of August 31st 1970. The pub had been taken over by Thomas Rowden Stanley Garside and his wide Cynthia, who was licensee, in 1969. The couple had been out for the evening and returned back to the pub after 10.30. Several customers who were in the bar of this small pub were about to witness a terrible event. They included lifelong friends of mine, John Madden and the late Terry Bottomley. The landlord who was behind the bar picked up a 12-bore shotgun which had been loaned to him by Joyce Wright's father to shoot rabbits with. He pointed it at his head and pulled the trigger, dying instantly from the severe injuries he sustained. This dreadful scene must surely have haunted those who witnessed the tragedy that night in the small hamlet of Boulderclough.The inquest was held at the Council Chambers in Hollins Lane, Sowerby Bridge, where the jury reached a verdict of suicide.

On a lighter note, John Madden who joined the West Yorkshire Constabulary in 1973 and became a coroner's officer while still a serving Police Constable has recently retired after 20 years in the job. He recalls one drinker fleeing through a rear window of the pub, in fear of being nabbed for after-hours drinking – he must have been pretty agile as the window would be a small one.

There are two public houses still in the village, the Church Stile Inn at the top of Sowerby New Road and next to the turn for Pinfold Lane; and the Rush Cart, formerly The Star Inn, is situated at the bottom of Well Head Lane, renamed in recent times as the pub plays a large part in the Rushbearing Festival held every September. The tradition of providing rushes for the church floors was revived in Sowerby Bridge and surrounding areas in 1977 after a break of more than seventy years. Mr Gary Stringfellow was responsible for the re-birth of this popular weekend festival, which is supported by locals and people from many areas who travel to attend the event.

The Star Inn, date unknown. Can you identify the structure on the corner?

The Star Inn was built by the Jennings family in 1798. The first landlord was Capt. Jennings, son of Stephen Jennings who was a provision dealer and supplied goods to the former workhouse situated at Bentley Royd in Sowerby New Road. When the captain died in 1800, the Star passed onto his wife, who ten years later married John Whiteley who was known as "John Almighty".

Portrait of John Almighty.

He was a Sowerby Parish Constable and used to preach from a pulpit (an old Post Boy's box) in an upper room at the pub: his ghost is said to haunt the building. In 1849 the pub and adjoining cottage, a slaughterhouse, butcher's shop and some outbuildings were put up for auction. The area measured about 346 square yards, and was described as formerly an encroachment that had been made from the Commons of Sowerby, the property of the Lord of the Manor. Following John Whiteley as landlord at the Star was William Firth of Stile, Sowerby. He sold the slaughterhouse, butcher's shop and some outbuildings on 6 July 1852 to John Nicholl who was a butcher. This part in 1868 was sold to John Rawson of Brockwell for £505, and in 1871 he purchased the Star Inn for £780. In early times Sowerby had a lock – up for offenders, perhaps for an overnight stay; also a Pinfold to hold any stray animals in, until reclaimed.

Lock-Up and Pinfold to the rear of the Star Inn (now The Rushcart).

Joe and Betty Kershaw moved from Oakworth near Keighley and took over the pub in 1954. Their son David remembers the piano in the snug, where customers would sing along to the music. This room was on the left as you walked into the pub – this was before alterations took place and the living quarters were moved upstairs. He also remembers the portrait of John Almighty being cleaned and hung on the wall of the taproom for some time. There was also a pulpit in the taproom at one time; later this was removed and stored in the stables out in the yard. This item was later discovered among items at Shibden Hall Folk Museum in Halifax.

At one time there were four public houses in Town Gate: The Shoulder of Mutton, The Blue Bell, The King's Head, which had a bowling green at the rear, and later became the Church Institute, and the Star Inn. At Boulderclough there was a public house called The King's Arms, now converted into cottages. The Shepherds' Rest at Hubberton, opposite the bus terminus, was known as The Riggin, also now converted into housing. The licensee was George Ward; he and his wife Lilian had two sons, Stuart and Peter. They took over at the pub in 1954. At Steep Lane the Travellers' Rest is still there, although now much changed and providing restaurant facilities and a trendy interior.

Ladies' outing to Blackpool c. 1957 leaving the Star Inn - David Kershaw (the landlord's son) kneeling at front. Una Berry (on left of lady at rear with hat) had won some cash and treated them to a day out.

Men's pub trip to Redcar Races 1952.

The following information was provided by Eleanor Mount, ex-landlady of The Church Stile Inn, Sowerby:

The population of Sowerby in 1810 was 4,051
The Church Stile Inn was rebuilt in 1884; it was only a beer house.
A full licence was granted in 1951.

Licensees from 1871 were:

Sarah Turner	1871 – 1880
James Nicholl	1880 – 1886
Jonathon Helliwell	1886 – 1901
Arthur Stead	1901 – 1906
Sam Lum	1906 – 1910
Edward Thomas	1910 – 1915
Arthur Crowther	1915 – 1924
Ellen Crowther	1924 – 1933
John Crowther	1933 – 1936
Laura Crowther	1936 – 1940
Joe Coley	1940 – 1957
John Neary	1957 – 1958
Stanley Fisher	1958 – 1961
John Mc Clouglon	1961 – 1965
Stanley Mount	1965 – 1984

Stan and Eleanor Mount were the longest serving landlords, completing over nineteen years at The Church Stile.

Stan and Eleanor Mount with Prince their Alsatian dog, 1970s (Evening Courier).

Mother in the park opposite the Church Stile Inn: the pub was decorated for the wedding of Charles & Diana in July 1981.

The small park opposite The Church Stile used to be larger and had three green benches, which were well used. Plenty of bushes and shrubs grew here and the borders of flowers and the grass were well attended by the council gardeners. Chains were attached to posts to the front and the side of the park and as children we used to sit on the spiky chains and swing backwards and forwards, somewhat uncomfortably! Up Queen Street built into the wall was a gents' urinal – if you look carefully you can see where the entrance has been bricked up. The top was open, and when we were playing hide-and-seek among the bushes in the park, we often peeped over the top of the urinal and the visiting gent below was totally unaware of our presence – unless, of course, someone began to snigger, then the game was "up". The area near the bus stop was the site of the former council "Town House" (before my time), used as a library, polling station and meeting room of the old Sowerby Local Board, and was also where the cannon and the village stocks were. I seem to remember when I was a child the stocks being across the road on the slope of grass on an area called Stocks Lane, so perhaps they were moved there at a later date. At one time in later years there was a substantial stone bus shelter with ladies' and gents' toilets included. This shelter provided good cover from the lashing rain and wintry weather experienced in Sowerby. The block was demolished after bouts of vandalism and none of the countless replacements have been as practical or attractive to look at. The drinking well above the bus stop was once a feature of the village but is sadly now in a poor state of repair. The well is engraved "John Rawson of Brockwell, died February 8, 1899" and is made of blue-grey and pinkish marble. The small top bowl was for people to take a drink from, using one of two small metal cups that hung from chains on the engraved tablet of the well. The lower well was for dogs and horses to drink from. It is now flagged over and in a poor condition.

Most of the houses and farms in the village of Sowerby were owned either by the Rawson family or the Stansfeld family. Our house at number 32, Town Gate was owned by the Rawsons and I remember going to Haugh End with my mother, walking down the narrow Back Lane (the footpath as it is today, by the side of the cricket field) down Piggy Lane to the office in the Mill House to pay the rent when it was due. Selwyn Rawson would mark up our rent book. Many years later the Rawsons sold off properties as they became vacant through local agent Walker Singleton. Our house in Pinfold Lane purchased in 1973 had been a Rawson property and, as it needed modernisation and upgrading, we were able to buy it at a time when building supplies were short. We took on the property which had been empty for some time and pulled out the small bath in the back bedroom cupboard, made a bathroom, and created a landing, also pulling out the black range in the kitchen before we started with the alterations. The gas lighting was replaced and electricity installed.

My childhood home and up to getting married at 32, Town Gate was in a block of three dwellings and had previously been a Conservative Club. Mr and Mrs Frank Barrett and Mr Armitage, Mrs Barrett's father, lived at No. 30 facing down the main road. Mr Barrett was a small man and he only had one arm. Their son Denis worked abroad, in the oil industry in the Persian Gulf. In later years they emigrated to Kogarah in New South Wales in Australia, where Denis and his family had moved to live. Next door to us lived Mr Milton and Mrs Ivy Smith; their house, which faced down to Town Farm, was called "Club House". My father and mother moved to No. 32 from further up the road; they had previously lived at "Green Cottage" at the bottom of Rooley Lane …

Rooley Lane, showing Green Cottage,
Rooley Lane Sunday School and Rooley Lane Chapel above.

and before that at Carr Lane, which is along Dob Lane and then down a track.

Carr Lane, 1945.

This area is now much changed with the demolition of buildings and modernisation of others. My brother David, seven years my senior, was born on 22nd June 1937 when mum and dad lived at Soyland before moving to Sowerby, so there had been quite a few house moves.

No. 32 Town Gate was a cold house with high ceilings and large windows. The ceiling in the living room was a wooden boarded one and there was a stone sink and a wooden draining board in one corner with a partition and curtain to close it off from the rest of the room. Large cupboards filled the recesses at either side of the grey-tiled fireplace. The wooden fire surround was unusual with a pillar on each side and a mirror in the centre. Our large rolltop writing desk had many pigeonholes, drawers and pull-out flat shelves but it took up a lot of room. The house had one main door facing up Sowerby and a sort of passageway with what was called the "kitchen", housing a gas stove, a wooden cupboard-cum-work table, a "bit rug" on the floor and a door which went through into my father's butcher's shop. There was not much room or encouragement to spend a great deal of time cooking in there! Upstairs we had two large bedrooms, each with ill-fitting sliding sash windows, which let in plenty of cold air in the winter weather. We were considered quite "modern" as a bathroom had been installed: many people were still visiting an outside toilet and some even had the old tub toilets. An open coal fire was our heating source; the coal delivery was deposited into the washhouse round in the back yard, as our house did not have a cellar. The cellar at

Club House was a large one, probably the main one when the building was used as a club. The washhouse was a stone building with three mangles, wash-tubs, a boiler to boil the "whites", possers and rubbing boards which were used to scrub badly-soiled items, in fact all the wash-day machinery for the three households. During the very cold winter weather, washdays must have been a terrible job and it was no wonder my mother used to get sore and chapped hands. This is when the Snowfire solid green healing block was used to heal the chaps and cuts she suffered from. Warmed and softened in front of the fire it was soothing and healing to her sore hands. Drying the clothes in front of the fire took ages and the windows would steam up. The ironing was done on the dining table, which would be covered with several thickness of folded sheet to make a smooth surface to iron on. The iron was electric but I seem to remember seeing a big iron with a compartment at the bottom to burn charcoal. Mother had a small sleeve-board that had been made by Trevor Dixon, a close family friend who was a joiner. The sleeve-board had been made for pressing my brother David's baby dresses and nightdresses. Baby boys used to wear them for the first few months of their lives; romper suits came in later. The sleeve-board continued to be used for a lot of other items, fiddly things such as puff sleeves and collars and lapels on blouses. Trevor also made my sledge which went very fast as it was a lightweight wood. I also had a cute little rocking chair, with an upholstered padded back and a separate upholstered cushion, and I used to love sitting in it and rocking back and forth, nursing my dollies. I had two super Gollies which had been handmade by a lady in Beechwood called Mrs Gledhill. They were dressed in brightly coloured clothes, smart jackets and trousers. She also used to come and do the washing for us when mother was working in the shop when I was younger. It felt good when all that washing and ironing was dealt with and back into the airing cupboard and drawers. When the better weather arrived the yard would be full of clothes blowing on the line. Mother used to get cross if the wind wrapped the clothes around the line; she would tut-tut a little, then trail round to the yard to pull them all straight, only to get back inside when the same thing would happen again! Mrs Smith also hung her washing in the yard, but Mrs Barrett's line stretched across the lane from her door to the gable end of No. 28 Town Gate.

As well as all the washday paraphernalia, the washhouse also had mysterious glass bottles containing bleach and ammonia. I remember taking the top off one of those bottles and inhaling, reeling backwards with eyes streaming – needless to say, I never did that again. The soap-powder boxes were stored in the house, as they needed to be kept dry. There was usually a box of Oxydol, Omo, Persil or Acdo in use. Dolly Blues were used for added whiteness I think, something magic contained in a muslin bag. There was another type that Mother used for the net curtains; this was a yellow bag, called "dolly cream". Hanging from the ceiling were some chains, connected to the stone floor. They were a reminder of earlier times when the washhouse had been a slaughterhouse. A poleaxe had been originally used to kill the beasts though this was replaced by humane killer in later times. Bob Holland, one of the earlier butchers, used to live at Town Farm nearby. His cows were reared in and grazed the surrounding fields, then slaughtered as required to supply the shop, providing fresh local meat for the village. My father ran the shop at one time with his brother Selwyn, when it was known as Smith Brothers. Later he used to run a taxi service. When the Co-op took it over, a butcher called Jack ran the shop. He was followed by Geoffrey Gledhill, who came into it in about 1947. And he was there until the butcher's moved into the house next to the Co-op lower down Town Gate in 1955 or '56. The shop then was taken over by Mr James and Mrs Freda Shaw of New Barton, Hubberton who ran Barton Electrics until retiring in January 1994. They did electrical contracting work and sold electrical goods, and radio and television repairs. Bob was the main contractor for the Sowerby Bridge Industrial Society and his wife Freda was the daughter of a master grocer. Their only daughter is called Beulah; I remember on her wedding day she forgot her bouquet and a journey had to be made back up to New Barton, Hubberton, to pick it up. Bob became a qualified hypnotherapist in the 1950s. They were always kind and helpful to my mother, who would take in any delivery for them that came when the shop was closed. The other butcher's and greengrocer's shop in Sowerby was opposite the Church Stile Inn, just below the bend. It was owned by Bob Steadman, who had a wooden leg, the result of an accident with a funeral vehicle. His wife Mary would help out in the shops. I remember when the shops and the cottages were demolished, there was a landslip and some of the large box-type graves in the bottom of St Peter's grave yard collapsed and bones were exposed. Screening was erected and workmen had to quickly sort the problem out.

Malan Ford outside the cottage, late 1940s, showing Sowerby New Road on the left.

My friend Malan Ford lived next to the shop with her dad and mum, who was Bob's sister. One of the dinner ladies at St Peter's Infants School used to live in one of the cottages around the back of Bob's shop at Stock's Lane; she was a large kindly person called Mrs Smith, who was always popular with the children at the school.

Friends and neighbours

Across the road from our house the Dixon family lived at 34, Highfield Place. There was Mr Stanley Dixon and Mrs Amy Dixon with children Pat and Terry. Next door was Miss Adel Kerridge at No. 36 and at the bottom of the street was Town Farm, where Mr and Mrs Jimmy Greenwood lived with their son Dennis. Mr Stanley Berry, the local painter and decorator, lived next door with his wife. In Queen Street (the one below ours) at No. 3 were Mr Fred and Mrs Alice Hartley, with sons David and Stuart. Mrs Firth (Mrs Hartley's mother) lived with them. Ernest Kerridge and his wife Daisy, with children Brenda, Margaret and John, lived next door. Their aunts Janet, Rachael and Susan lived next door to them.

Demolition of Nos. 31 – 45 Town Gate, 1962: view from rear of houses.

Facing our house there used to be a row of houses with an archway in the middle. Some were through houses and some were back-to-back. Pat and Terry's aunts Clarice and Florrie lived there and were at one time caretakers of the Providence Chapel. Florrie later married Wilson Sharp and moved into the house next door. The top house had an adjoining yard and some farm buildings; Mr and Mrs Frank Hanson lived here. Mr Hanson was a cattle dealer, and also kept pigs. A small man and rather rotund, he wore a waistcoat and had a watch-chain across his front. He was rather a "Tweedle Dee" type of character, contrasting to his taller and slimmer wife. The fields were accessible through a gate and a snicket leading onto "the delf" up the side of Haigh's Buildings. We used to play on the delf as children and the sloping fields were ideal for games of "roly poly" – we would roll over and over all the way to the bottom of the field. The delf had water falling down from quite a height and the place had an air of secrecy and peace about it. Here we would make daisy chains and hold a buttercup under a friend's chin to look out for the yellow reflection to prove that he or she liked butter. There were also dainty, delicate pale blue harebells growing there and pink clover that we used to pick and suck out the juice from the bottom of the petals. From the top of the field there was a stunning panorama of distant Wainstalls, Halifax and the Norland hillside. A footpath through the field led to a snicket and steps, which exited just below Peter Moore's farm. That field still exists but the council estates used up all the other fields.

Childhood friends were near neighbours Pat and Terry Dixon and David and Stuart Hartley, and have remained friends throughout my life. Sadly David died on August 30th 2003 in Portsmouth where he had been the licensee of the Graham Arms public house for some years but he came home to St Peter's to be buried in the graveyard. From about the age of three years I would totter round to David's house, negotiate the steep steps down into their yard and knock at the door to ask, "Is Dadie playing out?" He was a couple of years older than me, and Stuart two years younger. Their father Fred was connected with the pantomimes at the tennis club and the family attended St Peter's Church. His wife Alice was always immaculate in appearance. She was a tailoress and also a corsetiere for Spirella corsets as the black plaque at the front door informed everyone. She made lovely toffee, which was always a treat for us children. Mrs Firth (Mrs Hartley's mother) lived with them. I remember that she used to have a bed in the front room as her health deteriorated. She was always, like her daughter, very neat and tidy even in bed! Dr Morck called in to see her regularly. If I was ill in bed and needed a visit from the doctor, our house was the next call after the Hartleys. Usually it would be a bad case of a septic throat or tonsillitis that would lay me low as a child. I used to be terrified of "having to have them out", with the story of my father's tonsil removal at home on the kitchen table not helping very much. Mine were never removed, much to my relief, and as I grew older the problem lessened. If a home visit was necessary, my mother used to go into a sort of "over-drive" with the bed having to look just so, at least a clean pillow-slip put on, and the counterpane or eiderdown plumped up or straightened. There was a clean nightie for me to wear, my hair was brushed and combed, and I was told to "sit up straight", or rather was propped up against the pillows behind my back and shoulders. Perhaps the staircase needed a quick flick with the duster and what about the dressing-table and the tallboy? With all signs of dust removed, the curtains straightened, mother would peer out of the window looking towards the farm. When she spotted the doctor, leaving the Hartleys' house, usually driving a large car or in the warmer weather a sports car with the top down and a beautiful black Labrador dog sitting next to him, mother would disappear downstairs to greet him. Dr Harold Morck was an impressive figure of a man and, if he was wearing his sheepskin coat, he looked even larger. Stethoscope in one hand and his pad of prescriptions in the other, his first job was to have a look out of the two windows and to notice any object of interest in the bedroom. Finally he would come to the bedside to examine me, the little girl who never wanted to hear him say that I had to go into the hospital and have the tonsils removed. Luckily the big white penicillin tablets that he prescribed would usually help to get me better. David used to suffer from boils when he was growing up, usually around the collar area. Dr Morck used to ask: "Haven't you any hot water at your house?" – in other words, bathe them! Lions Ointment, which had a thick yellow consistency, was sometimes used "to draw things out"; it came in an unusual light wooden tub, stapled together and the wording poker-burnt onto the tub. It had a picture of a male lion on the lid and the tub was usually placed in the hearth near to the fire to soften the ointment before use.

If a visit to the surgery at Church Bank in Sowerby Bridge was necessary, the rather gloomy atmosphere was immediately apparent. Patients sat and waited on high-backed chairs which lined the walls, the only distraction being a large fish tank on one wall. The contents were a bit of a mystery as the water in the tank was very discoloured and I cannot remember seeing much activity within the murkiness. After being seated for a while, a small brown wooden box-like door would open on the far wall, and Miss Buckley, the doctor's receptionist, would appear. Her hairstyle – perfect, eyebrows plucked to a neat arched shape. She would take a quick glance at the latest person to enter the waiting room and without a word find their medical records. When it was your turn to go through the soundproof door to see Dr Morck, she would hand the records to you to give to the doctor. Mother would have been into the separate examination room a few times (thank goodness I didn't have to). She had to have several hernia operations; it seems that our family are fated with them! Mine (two) came later in life, my brother also has had a few repairs and some of my late uncles were sufferers too. Before I was born, Mother had a hernia operation and was in hospital for two weeks before being allowed home. She was carried on a stretcher and taken upstairs to bed, where she had to stay for another couple of weeks. Quite a contrast to methods used today when you can be operated on and home within several hours.

Dr Morck, a qualified pilot with a larger-than-life personality, lived next to the surgery at Orrell House, which still has a front gate into Wharf Street. He had a car accident at Poole Bank near Harrogate and sustained serious injuries. The other doctors in Sowerby Bridge were Dr John McKelvey whose surgery was at the corner of Station Road in Sowerby Bridge and who used to visit local mills to check the health of the girls working there, Dr Jollie who had his surgery in the Bull's Head yard, and Dr McCauley in the old Tuel Lane. There was also a Dr Gallagher.

Another dreaded visit was to the school dentist at Allen House in Station Road, Sowerby Bridge. Teeth were examined at school, and appointments made for you to attend the clinic there. It used to be an ordeal for me as a youngster as needles were my worst fear and unfortunately my teeth usually required some treatment or other as I was lacking in calcium, I remember being told. When I reached eleven years old my mother decided to move me to Mr Jackson's dental surgery in Tuel Lane. Now the nightmare of visits to the dentist really began. This cold large Victorian house was most unwelcoming and I dreaded my appointments there. Having to have my front teeth filled by this dentist scared me and made me afraid of going to the dentist for many years. Injections felt as though they were going up into my head and the needles then were not the fine ones that are used today. I should have been fitted with a brace to straighten my front teeth, but it was never suggested, so I have smiled a crossover smile most of my life. Fortunately dentists are much less frightening today thanks to modern equipment and a gentler approach.

Pupils were also sent to Allan House for sunray treatment. Beryl Waddington, my school friend, was sent there for the lamp treatment, stripping off to the waist to absorb the health-giving rays and wearing goggles to protect the eyes. Harry Nelson from Pollit Avenue also went there for treatment; maybe he also contracted Tuberculosis, and I do know that he was sent to Norway at some point for recuperation and the benefits of the good clean air to breathe into his lungs. Another visitor to the school was the nit nurse who came to check for head lice among the pupils. You always knew when someone had them as they would be issued with a note for a lotion from the chemist. We always had a fine toothcomb in use at home, but the worse scenario that happened to me was getting a head full of horseflies! Visiting Stones Farm one morning to watch one of my father's horses being groomed, I was standing in the doorway to the stable, wearing a little knitted bonnet on my head, unaware that as the grooming continued and the horse was looking much better I was accumulating some unwanted visitors in my woolly head gear. Back at home on removal of the bonnet my mother was shocked to find my blonde head full of horseflies. She hastily consulted our neighbour Mrs Barrett, who came round to inspect my problem and advised mother to use a liberal amount of vinegar and to brush it through my hair to get rid of the blighters! After the rather messy and unpleasant job, my head was clear of the flies. I feel itchy just remembering and writing about it! Some of the children at school developed ringworm on their scalps and this was treated by the application of Gentian Violet and usually the hair would be shaved off in that area so it was quite visible with the purple area showing up brightly on the scalp.

School days

The first school I attended was St Peter's C of E near the church. It is now the Sunshine Private Day Nursery for children under five and also used as a community centre. The school pupils moved to the newly-modernised Newlands Junior School, that underwent a £800,000 refurbishment to create the Sowerby Village School and merged together infants and junior pupils under one roof. It opened in September 2002 to pupils, but the official opening by local musical star Emma Williams was in April 2003.

If I remember correctly, I started school at the age of five, walking the short distance down the road from my home. Sitting on the small chairs in Mrs E. Albrighton's class, it was here that friendships with Beryl Waddington and Christine Brooke were formed and continued through our schooling and up to the present time. Reading my school report of June 1950 when I was six, there were 41 pupils in the class and my attendance was marked as "very good". Our subjects were reading, arithmetic, painting and drawing, handwork, singing, poetry and nursery rhymes, as well as writing, PT, games and scripture. Mrs Albrighton was the class teacher and the headmaster was Mr F J Wright. Their comments were added to the bottom of the report, which then had to be signed by a parent to prove it had been read and returned to school to be checked for the parents' signature.

My report of 1951, when I was in Class 2, shows that my teacher Miss C M Taylor was pleased with my work; this lady is well into her nineties and today lives in a home in West Vale. By the time I was in Mr Proctor's class of 36 scholars I was just over eight. What a good teacher Mr Proctor was: patient and kind, he really did bring out the best in his pupils.

Myself – June 1953.

It was not so in the next class of Mr A Ingham's which was such a contrast that my report for the year ended June 1953 was not at all encouraging. Mr Ingham's comments have stuck with me all my life: "Her late entry into this class has been I feel a handicap rather than an asset. It has been very difficult to fit her in." Perhaps if Mr Ingham had been a little more patient in explaining certain things, rather than throwing the wooden-backed blackboard rubber at pupils, we would have all done better. Much of my time seemed to be spent facing the bookcase doing absolutely nothing, rather a negative and pointless procedure he seemed quite fond of putting his pupils through.

One highlight of his classes was that when the fancy took him he would take the pupils across the road and into St Peter's Church. We would go up to the area where the bell ropes hang, sit cross-legged on the floor and he would read to us. This was a treat and we used to enjoy this change from the normal routine. Mr Ingham was a tall man with thinning sandy hair and he used to wear a sports jacket that had leather patches sewn onto the elbows. I think he used to walk up Pinfold Lane to get to the school, so maybe he lived down in the valley somewhere.

Other teachers were Mrs Hall and Mrs Newton whose husband was the vicar at Steep Lane Chapel and who lived at the Manse with their daughters Ruth and Helen and son John. The school caretaker, Mr Nicholl, lived in the house behind the school building. He would attend to the boiler house next to the front porch entrance, which was reached by going down a flight of stone steps. There was a gaping opening across the top and as children we used to jump across this space. There would have been a nasty accident if anyone had fallen down the gap.

Mrs Smith, a large, cheery lady from Stocks Lane, was a dinner lady, also Mrs Paley from St Peter's Avenue (Adrian's mother), Mrs Cardwell from Pollit Avenue, Mrs Easton from Finkle Street and, in later years, Mrs Jowett who lived in the cottage next to the school. Mrs Tetley was a long-serving dinner lady at both St Peter's and Newlands schools. These ladies served out the school dinners which, I think, were prepared somewhere in Sowerby Bridge and then transported up to the school in containers. At that time I was probably entitled to have free dinners as my mother was supporting David and me on her own. There was always a bit of a stigma being in the possession of a free dinner ticket and queuing separately for food.

At a quarter to two the large brown, bakelite radio would be switched on and we would sit cross-legged on the floor for "Listen with Mother", most likely nodding when the presenter inquired, "Are you sitting comfortably?" The radio was also in use for "Movement to Music" when we would prance around the floor being as light as a fairy or clomping heavily as a giant. I think when we were very young we may have had a little rest in the afternoon, as a refresher. Nature walks were often taken and we were introduced to the many types of trees and leaves that we passed on Dean Lane, usually bringing back items to copy and press or draw in our nature books. Sometimes we would get our sketching materials and walk up to the almshouses to sit and draw them, showing their ornate style and the grassed area in front of them. We also used to do country dancing and at one time I was sitting on the floor with my hands behind me when John Madden, who was wearing clogs, trod on the middle finger of my right hand. I have had a bump there ever since, but the other bumps on my fingers are now of the arthritic type!

Another time all the pupils were taken into the playground to watch an eclipse. I remember it going very dark, then getting lighter again.

Class Photograph with teacher Mrs Newton, Saint Peter's Infants School, Sowerby 1953
Back Row, left to right: Alan Howarth, Donald Bower, Christopher Sheppard, Terry Manning, Dennis Hobson, Roy Butterworth, Colin Drake, Colin Midgley, Tony Murphy, Adrian Paley, Christopher Brocklehurst, Andrew Mallinson.
Middle Row: Terry Dixon, Raymond Murphey, Rodney Broadbent, Rose Helliwell, Christine Rose, Pauline Halstead, Dorothy Gill, Christine Saltonstall, David Kelly, John Madden, Stuart Walker, Teacher, Mrs Newton.
Front Row: Elaine Whitehead, Margaret Pickles, June Mottershead, Beryl Waddington, Jean Smith (myself), Jean Brayshaw, Celia Jones, Christine Brooke, Valerie Dennis, Pauline Brown.
Front: Billy Thorpe, Grenville Parkin, Gordon Taylor.

There were air-raid shelters in two locations, one across from the top end of the yard on the Dean Lane side, and another just about opposite Mr Nicholls' house. We played skipping games and tig at playtime and a handbell was rung to get us to line up for entry back into our lessons.

Milk was delivered in small bottles, for our daily consumption, though it used to make me feel sick. The milk would be frozen solid in winter, so the crates would be put against the pipes to thaw out and the resulting tepid mush was awful. We were also given a daily capsule of cod liver oil to provide us with a source of vitamins. At Christmas we made paper trimmings and Chinese lanterns to decorate the classrooms and went over to services at the church. We decorated the classroom walls with our powder paint pictures and used flour and water as paste to stick things together.

During my time at St Peter's there was a serious health scare. My friend Malan Ford contracted typhoid fever when she was about eight or nine years old. Malan was born in February 1945 and used to live with her parents John Frederick and Ruby Mary (née Steadman) at a cottage next door to her uncle Bob's greengrocer and butcher's shop on the bend just below Stocks Lane. The family later moved into a newly-built council house on Newlands Avenue. Malan had been on a family outing and picnic to Shibden Park and had to pay a visit to the toilet there. She later became ill and was diagnosed with typhoid fever. This was most serious at the time and Malan almost lost her life. Typhoid fever is an acute sometimes epidemic disease of the digestive system. It is caused by Salmonella typhi transmitted in contaminated water or food. The symptoms include fever, headache, constipation, sore throat, a cough and a skin rash. When I met up with Malan in October 2004 for a coffee and a chat, she told me about this awful time in her life but could not remember the exact year of the illness. Dr Gallagher from Sowerby Bridge was the family GP and my friend Beryl Waddington remembers seeing the ambulance coming to take Malan away to the isolation hospital in Leeds. She was put into an attic room fitted with a half-gate across the door. Visitors had to stand beyond the gate and throw any gifts brought for the patient onto the bed, thus avoiding any contact. The gifts were later destroyed. One side effect of the disease was that Malan's hair fell out. Her mother and her brother Allan also contracted a mild strain of the disease; they were treated in hospital at Halifax. Malan learned to recognise the various nurses' footsteps during her stay, and recalls a nurse Dyson. She had to use her own plate and cutlery and after she returned home, the health officer used to call to test her and see if she was clear of infection. This event caused a change in the hygiene procedures at St Peter's School and all children were instructed to bring a small hand towel and to thoroughly wash their hands after a visit to the outside toilets at the school. The towels used to hang on hooks next to a sink just inside the side entrance to the school. Malan was away from her schooling for about eighteen months – on her return she went over to the newly-opened Newlands School and joined Mrs Cotton's class. Her hair grew again and she was able to resume her dancing – in later years also danced with her daughter Michaela.

The new school built just below St Peter's was Newlands County Primary School, and would provide brand new modern premises for the pupils. It was built to accommodate 280 children and was designed for junior and infant children, but was adapted for juniors, the infants remaining at St Peter's. The interior was bright and light with classroom doors painted in different colours for easy identification by the children. The assembly hall and dining hall were separated by a folding partition and these folded back to create a large hall when needed. There was a long hatch from kitchen to dining-room, thus providing easy access for the serving of school dinners. The modern light fittings resembled flying saucers, the parquet floors made a smooth contrast to the old floor-boarding at St Peter's and the luxury of a central heating system was much appreciated during Sowerby's cold winter weather. The head teacher was Mr Raymond Milnes who held the position until his retirement in 1973 which was also the last year of the old West Riding Education Authority. The official opening of the school on April 30, 1955 was carried out by the Rt. Hon. J Chuter Ede CH JP DL MP, President of the County Councils Association. Mrs Cotton was in charge of the school choir and I remember practising the songs selected for the school's opening ceremony. We performed Handel's Minuet from *Berenice* ("Come see where golden-hearted Spring"), "Stay in Town" ("Little White") which was a very modern piece, "Rio Grande", ("O say were you ever in Rio Grande? Way down Rio") and the Eriskay Love Lilt ("Vere me oho ro van o, vere me oh o ro van e").

Moving across to Newlands and into the top class taught by Mr Proctor, I remember my weak subject was arithmetic, especially mental arithmetic. There was much frantic working out on the back of my hand or a quick desperate glance at Beryl for an answer but my marks were not very good in this subject. Peter Ward, Norman Clarke and Frank Albrighton (son of the teachers Mr and Mrs Charlie Albrighton) were the brainy ones in the class and they passed the eleven plus examination to go to the Grammar School in Sowerby Bridge. If I remember correctly, Irene Bruce and Hazel Clarke were among the few girls who passed but it was my fate to start at Sowerby New Road Girls Secondary Modern School in the summer of 1955 along with my friends Beryl Waddington and Christine Brooke. This next period in our education has been recorded in my booklet "A Personal View".

Ben Ackroyd

Sowerby had many characters and Ben Ackroyd and his brother Fred certainly fitted into that category. They spoke in such broad Yorkshire accents that some people had difficulty understanding them. I spoke to Ben about his memories in 2002 when he was 87 in his flat at Rawson Wood. Ben's schooling at St Peter's began in 1919 when he was five. The head teacher was Mr Frank Fielding Hollas and other teachers were Miss Blaymires, who taught the baby class, Miss Garnett who was rather frightening in appearance to a young child, strict and severe, Miss Tidswell who married a butcher in Town Hall Street, Sowerby Bridge, and Miss Normanton, the teacher of standard four. Ben wore clogs on his feet, a grey jersey and short grey trousers, a tie and a school cap. To write, a slate and chalk were used. The playground games included cricket, football, tig and hide-and-seek. One day the pupils went into the playground to look up into the sky at an aeroplane – it was the first one they had ever seen! Miss Garnett sent Ben on a regular errand to the Co-op up the road to buy one pound of Yorkshire mixtures every Friday and the sweets were then shared out between the children. If there was a sweet left over Ben was allowed to have it for doing the errand. He remembers the cane being used as a punishment. He received it for sledging down Pinfold Lane one lunchtime and being late in returning to school. He was also caned for painting some eggs that had been on the teacher's desk. Prizes were awarded for tidy work and one of the books Ben received was called "100 Things a Boy Can Make". Ben and his sister Nellie may be the oldest surviving ex-pupils of St Peter's School.

His family used to live at 6, Rooley Lane, and the children were called Louie, Walter, Nellie, Willie, Frank, Fred, Ethel, Ben, Florence and Mary was the youngest. Ben and Fred moved into a cottage in Rooley Lane Chapel yard in 1978; the two brothers were never married. His sister Nellie (Robinson) celebrated her 100th birthday on January 25th 2007.

Fred worked at Sagar Richards and used to walk there and back home again after his shift. The sound of his clogs on the road surface and his whistling could be heard as he walked past for his 6am start from our bedrooms at Town Gate. Before leaving home he would have cooked and eaten a full breakfast to set him up for the day. Fred and Ben cooked and baked healthy meals. Ben worked for Harry Howarth at Fields Farm, Hubberton, as a farmer's man; he also worked at Quickstavers Farm, Stanhope Farm, and Shade at Turvin Cross. He had learned to milk a cow by hand by the time he was nine years old at Red Brink at Hubberton. He was able to milk eight cows in an hour sitting on a three-legged stool and using a finger and his thumb to squirt the warm milk into a bucket called a "piggin" which had a lip that rested on the milker's knees. He never used a modern milking machine but told me that he had been kicked off the stool many a time by an awkward beast! At haymaking time Ben always wore a shirt, tie, jacket and flat cap, never stripping off to work in the fields even in the hottest of weather. The grass was cut by a cutting machine pulled by a horse. This was followed by hand raking and the hay was left to dry for approximately two days. Next it was turned over by hand, shaken through by a hand fork into windrows, two long rows which were then forked by hand onto the hay cart, and this would again be pulled by a horse. Working from the back to the front to load the wagon, one would start at the back then fill in the corners and work forward to balance the load and finally secure with a rope. Then it was transported into the barn to be stored for the animals to consume during the winter months. This method seems rather painstaking compared with today's much speedier cutting of the grass and then machine-wrapping the large rolls in polythene. The old method was, in my opinion, a more "country style" event and perhaps more helpful in supporting certain breeds of our birds and assisting their survival.

Ben finished with farming in 1946 and went wagon driving for Peel's at Mearclough where they made sectional buildings. He remained there for three and a half years before going to work at Wadsworth's Paints at Pear Street. He drove all over the country on various journeys, sometimes staying away for a few nights. He delivered paint to London County Council at one time. When the motorways came, Ben decided he wasn't interested in driving into London in a day and back home again, so he decided to leave. He went to work at Sagar Richards at Luddenden Foot until he retired aged 64. Ben also used to cut the grass using a scythe at the almshouses with farmer Sidney White. One of Ben's talents is being able to yodel – he used to practise as he walked over the tops at night time! He wouldn't oblige when I requested a sample of his yodelling but how I wish I could have heard him one calm still summery night as he walked along Ratten Row! Ben learnt to drive in a Morris Cowley bull-nosed car when he was twelve years old in a field up at Rooley Farm. He practised his reversing to park the car in between two bricks. The vehicle was used on the farm in the hayfield and, at night with the lights on, it was used to deliver milk.

Rocking horses

Standing in front of David's bedroom window facing up Town Gate there was a large dapple-grey rocking horse, visible to all who walked down the main road. It was not unusual for people to knock on the door and ask if it was for sale. My father had bought it from one of his contacts, and this horse "Silver", as I called him, provided hours of enjoyment and adventure for me and my friends. Fitted with a cowboy saddle and stirrups, a blonde mane and tail, he stood on a large wooden stand with a bar on either side to stand on, to mount him. The only problem was that the faster that you rocked, the more the stand would lift off the floor and return with a bit of a thud. This was not much fun for Geoffrey Gledhill working in the butcher's shop below the bedroom. He must have put up with the thuds on many occasions because everyone wanted to have a go on Silver. Over the years his mane became shorter and thinner as a favourite pastime for me was to get a brush and comb, curlers and crimpers, to make waves and give him a hairdressing session. Usually I would plait his long tail and tie hair ribbons on, then when I let the plaits out his tail had become nice and wavy. I also used to sneak in mother's Amami wave set, a blue setting lotion (their slogan used to be, "Friday night is Amami night") to give an extra special hairdo. Many happy hours were spent playing with Silver, who now resides at the Rocking Horse Museum in Fangfoss near York.

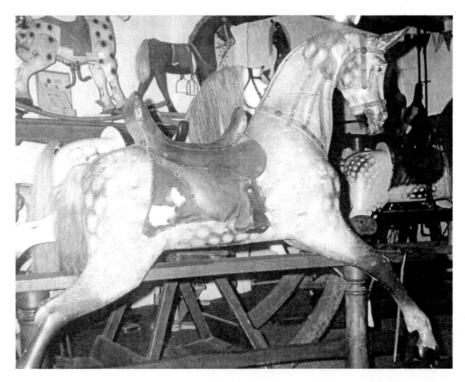

Silver at Fangfoss.

50

When mother moved house to a flat across the road at 49b, Town Gate, my brother David stored the rocking horse for many years in his garage premises at Park Road, Elland. Silver was later moved off in a horsebox to live (on loan) with other rocking-horses of all shapes and sizes and conditions at Fangfoss. There was no restoration work done on Silver as the museum prefers to display the horses as found. His lower jaw had been broken off for many years and several attempts at sticking it back on again failed. When Silver arrived at Fangfoss it was discovered that he was minus one of his glass eyes but fortunately the missing item was found among the sweepings when the garage floor was being cleaned after the horse had been removed. This was sent to be replaced at the museum. From information in a *Rocking Horse* magazine it appears that he was originally from Gamages store in London and was described as a "Bronk" safety hobby horse registered number Ty 467,670. It was originally made to the store's own designs and cost around 75/- to purchase then. It appears that it would cost £3,500 to buy an original horse today and £2,500 for a copy, which shows how much some of these items have increased in value and become very collectable. He is displayed with other horses, including a couple from schools within the Halifax area, for at one time it appears that rocking horses were part of school equipment. The *Halifax Courier*'s "Flashback" of October 5th 2000 featured a photograph of the infant class at Sowerby New Road Elementary School, as it was then known, complete with a dapple-grey rocking horse and two small pupils sitting astride it. This dated from 1922. When I visited the school during the '90s the rocking horse was still there but now painted black. It was in the late eighteenth and early nineteenth centuries that rocking horses on bow rockers became popular with wealthy parents to teach their children a sense of balance and to gain confidence on the back of a horse. The dappled grey was the standard finish from about 1850 to the present day. In 1880 the swing-iron or safety stand came in and replaced the more precarious bow rockers. Carved from pine in a hollow box construction and mounted on hardwood legs, the horse was then covered in gesso, a plaster-like substance, and then hand painted and varnished. The leather tack and horsehair mane and tail were then added. We have visited Fangfoss to see Silver with his new friends and the Rocking Horse Shop and Museum make an interesting outing for families.

There was an open fireplace in David's bedroom and sometimes when it was very cold during the winter mother would light a fire in the grate. It brought such a warm feel to the room and the chimney used to "draw very well", as mother put it. Dad once brought a black cat home, probably from a farm he had visited. It was rather wild and, though he had it in a sack, it shot out, up the staircase into David's room and straight up the chimney – luckily there wasn't a fire lit at the time. The cat eventually came down and we soon tamed him. Sooty lived with us for several years although he did go missing for a long period and we thought that we'd seen the last of him. After what seemed weeks he came home looking very thin and scraggy – we think he had been locked in the chapel across the road.

There were usually animals around at home. At one time hens were kept in the backyard and I think we had a turkey. I called one of the hens Limping Lizzie because she was lame and her foot turned under. David used to have a goat called Chocolate (before I can remember). It used to come into the house and follow my mother upstairs! Our dogs were a black and white cur (sheepdog) called Shep and a black and tan Manchester terrier called Tiny who used to go underneath the sideboard when there was a thunderstorm. The noise upset him so he probably felt safe there. One of my cats, Tiger, was almost human and seemed to understand everything I said to it. Dressed in a doll's nightie and wearing a bonnet, he would recline under the covers in my doll's pram and be pushed around like a baby. He also used to get into bed with me, to snuggle down and go to sleep, head on pillow. This wasn't very hygienic so mother would turf him out. I was devastated one day to return home from school to find him dead on the grass. He was not externally in a mess but he had a shell-like protrusion from one of his eyes so maybe had sustained head and internal injuries from being hit by a vehicle on the road and crawled into the grass to die. I remember running to meet my mother off the bus as she returned from work to tell her about my cat, with tears streaming down my face. It didn't help matters when his body was removed to be cremated on the boiler down at the farm – more tears again!

Mother worked for several years in Sowerby Bridge at Valkyrie Products whose premises were above the Tu-blar workshop opposite the bottom of the old Tuel Lane. Customers went in through some large wooden doors, up a wooden staircase to the shop floor, rang the bell and then waited to be admitted by a member of the staff. There was a large area full of wood in various shapes and sizes and stages and a right turn into the main workshop area. The business was run by Mr Spencer Fletcher and his son Jack whose wife Marjorie also worked there. The firm produced very attractive display and studio furniture. They also made reproduction picture and mirror frames, lamp stands and beautifully decorated bedroom furniture. One of their specialities was Adam- and William and Mary-style fireplace surrounds or mantels, made in wood and Gesso, an old Italian craft done entirely by hand. It was not intended to be a substitute for wood carving but the finished article gave that appearance. These items were usually sprayed cream and the ornate mouldings later gilded. I usually visited the workshop to see my mother after a trip to the dentist in Tuel Lane. I would try to slurp a pot of tea and eat something soft as my mouth would be numb from the dreaded injections. During those lunchtimes before returning to school in Sowerby New Road, I was able to watch the methods used to heat up the putty-like substance of glue, resin and raw linseed oil before it was pressed into the desired mould to create perhaps a floral design or leaf shape – the acanthus leaf featured in many of the decorations. During a twelve-month period the firm would use about seven and a half hundredweight of Gesso. The firm had to hand about 1,000 moulds, mainly designs from the Georgian and Regency periods, some of them used on a regular basis and some only very occasionally. When the individual mould had been filled with the Gesso, it would be would then turned over onto the workbench and left to set. A very sharp knife was then required to thinly and carefully slice the floral or leaf shape off. These finely sliced decorations were used to enhance the legs, curves and edges of the different styles of reproduction furniture that Valkyrie made. From being soft in the early stage the Gesso would set rock-hard once applied to the furniture item. Spraying the furniture took place in a separate area and masks were worn. It was interesting to see the various stages of work that the items of furniture were in. Many of the finished products were exported overseas and several staff, men and women, were employed there in this creative work. Edward Craven (Eddie) was taken to the firm by his mother when he left Haugh Shaw School at the age of fifteen. He was set on as a junior apprentice cabinetmaker at the rate of around £1-35 per week. He remembers having a close encounter with a chisel when he was working on a lathe with some wood frames. The chisel jammed in the machine, then flew out and hit him in the solar plexus. Luckily the handle, and not the chisel, end hit him. He was winded but managed to lean over and switch the machine off. Little attention was paid to the victim who then carried on with his work. Eddie joined The Duke of Wellington's regiment and had a long career with the army. He retired as Warrant Officer and now lives in Colchester.

There was a door from the workshop leading out onto a flat roof overlooking the River Calder. The building had been a billiards hall and then in use by the local Army cadets before the firm took it over in 1945. I think all this building has now been converted to apartments. The Tub-lar works produced a very different type of furniture – as the name suggests it was tubular metal furniture and fittings for offices, factories, canteens and domestic use. Not glamorous but this furniture was practical and sturdy. These two furniture manufacturers right next to each other in Sowerby Bridge could not have been more contrasting in the type of furniture they were producing.

Mother used to also work at the Church Stile Inn when Eleanor and Stanley Mount were the licensees. She was a cleaner there, working part-time for them from 1966 until 1981. She also worked for Eleanor in the fish and chip shop during 1974. She enjoyed working for Stan and Eleanor and they remained close friends for many years. Stan was renowned for his hanging baskets full of colourful blooms that hung outside the pub.

Characters

On Saturday mornings, a single-decker bus would pull up down at the farm – but not to pick up passengers. This was a green Bedford, an ex-London County Council school bus which had been converted to hold various household goods for sale. The driver, Brian Oldfield, would ring a large bell out of his window to announce his arrival and I would run down with my mother to see what he had for sale that day. There was a large selection of goods to choose from – pots and pans, sweeping brushes large and small, soap, dusters, firewood in bundles and paraffin to measure out, everything needed in the home. He also sold white and yellow donkey stones: these were used along the edges of doorsteps, and completed the task of "mapping out". Mother usually did this chore on a Saturday morning. The doorstep was scrubbed and the flags swilled with hot water, using a besom brush. People used to take great pride in the appearance of their doorsteps, and the outside of their homes. Brian had different routes on weekdays but always did the same route on Saturdays when he carried the most paraffin that day. He continued to provide this service for thirty years and then went on to drive buses for the corporation. He lived at Steps Lane in Sowerby Bridge then as he does today.

Mr Stanley Berry, who lived next door to the farm at No. 5, Queen Street, was a local painter and decorator. He employed Mr Wilson who lived at Well Head, higher up Sowerby. While Mr Wilson was always chewing gum, Mr Berry always seemed to have a cigarette in his mouth and would talk to you without removing it, sending ash and sparks flying. He did not own a car or any form of transport so he either walked or used the bus to get to his jobs. Wearing white overalls and an old trilby hat, carrying rolls of wallpaper tied up with string and slung over his shoulder, he would set off in a morning to work. Mother thought he was a "dirty worker" because of the smoking, and he tended to not clear up very well, but if any wallpapering or painting needed doing it was usually Mr Berry who got the job. I remember once when he had completed a job in our living room, my mother discovered that a section of wallpaper next to one of the windows was upside down. She was very annoyed and went down to report the error to him. He came up to the house to do an inspection and told mother, "It'll not show when the curtains are put back." Needless to say the offending piece of paper remained upside down! He once did some work down at St George's Church at Quarry Hill. The interior featured some beautiful fretworked wood screening with heraldic shields displayed. When he was renewing some of the items with paint he decided to change the colours used on them, which wasn't the correct thing to do! I'm not sure if they were ever returned to their original hues. The little garden at the side of the Berrys' house always had a good supply of rhubarb which was regularly "raided" by us children. We used to get quite a bit of tummy-ache after devouring the tart sticks.

Mrs Berry was a lovely lady. She worked as an usherette at the Odeon cinema in Broad Street, Halifax, and used to wear a burgundy-coloured uniform. Sadly their son Colin had learning disabilities and was away in a home. As a child I remember hearing that if ever anything happened to Colin, then Mrs Berry would leave her husband Stanley. When Colin eventually died, it wasn't long before one Sunday morning a large removal van pulled up outside their house. Mother had seen it arrive so we both went upstairs into our bedroom to watch what was happening from the window. Boxes and carrier bags were loaded into the van. Then Mrs Berry emerged from the porch with Ming, her Pekinese dog, tucked under her arm. She got into the front passenger seat and left Sowerby to go to the coast where her sister lived. Neula Lynch, who also worked at the Odeon, thinks Mrs Berry went to Fleetwood and later worked at a cinema there. Mr Berry continued to live in the same house until his death.

Mr Milton Smith and his wife Ivy next door at Club House were very kind to me throughout my childhood. Their only son Raymond had married Elizabeth (Betty) Pezzet from Old Hall at Field House and went to live and work in Norwich. There was always a birthday present, Christmas present, and a souvenir brought back from their holidays, day trips and outings for me. When I was going on a school visit to France, coins were saved up for me in a biscuit barrel on their sideboard, to help towards my spending money. Milton Smith worked at W P Eglin's at Globe Works, Victoria Road in Sowerby Bridge. They produced "contemporary furniture". He joined the firm on leaving school, and worked there for 57 years, first as a labourer, then a foreman and finally a traveller for the firm, ending up as the head representative. His service to the firm was only interrupted when he served in the Army in the First World War. He drove a grey Triumph "Mayflower" model car which he used to park in the backyard. He also was a regular traveller to Ireland by plane on business trips – quite unusual in those days. Mrs Ivy Smith used to enjoy going with him on his visits to Leeds and they would have lunch in Lewis's. She was a very large lady, but always happy and singing around the house. As she had swollen legs and difficulty walking, the only type of shoes she could wear were a flattish, round-toed style with a strap fastening onto a buttonhole across the top of her foot. She loved ironing and would hum and sing as she worked at a large table covered with a padded cloth. She made pounds of jam and I remember the table being full of jars and the big pan of jam on the gas stove waiting to reach "setting point". The cooker was by the side of the fire in the living room, later to be moved into the passage. The sink was housed in a large cupboard on the other side of the fireplace. There was a lot of wasted space in the house, a long back passage, huge space up the staircase and a big landing. A long narrow passage housed a flush toilet but they didn't have a bath or a washbasin. There was also a large attic and cellar and this building was most certainly the centre of the former Conservative club. When Mrs Smith died in 1969, Mr Smith was very lonely living alone. He made contact with a friend from the past and when he retired in 1972, he married a lady called Nancy who lived in Scarborough and spent his final years there with her and her son, dying at the age of 87.

Club House was bought by Eric and Christine Senior, when Mr Smith left. Later when 32, Town Gate was auctioned on June 27th, 1979 they bought the house where I had been born. When Bob Shaw retired from his electrical business in 1994, they also purchased the shop at auction.

When the Barretts moved out of No. 30 to emigrate to Australia in 1962, Donald and Jean Horne moved in and still live there, as do Eric (local electrician) and Christine next door.

My kind friends next door were one of the first households to own a television set. We certainly never owned one and my mother wouldn't get one until much later in her life. She called them "Time wasters", although I really didn't know what she meant by that remark. I was invited to be a guest to watch children's television next door from 5pm to 6pm each day and this routine continued for several years. I vividly remember the delights of "All Your Own", hosted by Huw Weldon, seeing the Kalin Twins perform "When" which went on to be a hit record, Eamonn Andrews hosting "Crackerjack" and giving out pens as prizes to the winners and cabbages to those who answered a question incorrectly. Drop anything and you were "out". Another favourite was "Champion the Wonder Horse", a series first broadcast in 1955 and set in the American South West. Produced by Gene Autry, it told the adventures of Ricky North, his wonder stallion Champion and faithful dog Rebel. The theme tune was later recorded by Frankie Lane. I also recall the Cisco Kid with his side-kick Pancho and the Lone Ranger, played by Clayton Moore and his Indian friend Tonto, played by an actor with the unforgettable name of Jay Silverheels. Then there were the episodes of Billy Bunter's adventures at Greyfriars School, Heidi, the little girl who was looked after by her grandfather on a mountain top in Switzerland, "Anne of Green Gables" and "Whirligig", a slapstick comedy show with Charlie Drake and Jack Douglas. I also remember the Children's Newsreel, the little girl on the test card and the "potter's wheel" piece of film shown if there was time to spare between programmes. I would sit and watch these programmes while Mr and Mrs Smith ate their tea together at the table. Usually I would be asked if I would like anything to eat and most likely it would be something home-made. On taking my leave I would always say, "Thank you for having me". As I grew older, if there was anything on the television in the early evening they thought I would be interested in watching, one of them would knock on the wall with a wooden spoon, and round I would go, through the gate and along the path which ran underneath our window to join them at the "grown up" time. It was usually a ballet (I was attending dancing class at the time) or perhaps a variety show such as "Sunday Night at the London Palladium" or a circus. The other people who had a television were the Greenwoods at the farm and Berrys next door to them. Sometimes my friends and I were invited in to these houses to watch if there was something suitable on.

Mother and I went up to the home of her sister (Auntie Ethel and Uncle John Jerrett) at Whiteley Terrace, along Bar Lane in Ripponden, to watch the Coronation of Queen Elizabeth II in June 1952. They were quite "posh" and had a 12-inch Bush television which was housed in a wooden polished cabinet with doors. There were always Macintosh's Quality Street sweets to eat and Cusson's Imperial Leather soap in the bathroom at Auntie Ethel's house (we only had the more common Palmolive soap at home). I remember when a soap called Breeze came on sale and we had a coupon put through the letterbox to try it but mother thought that it was too "searching" for the skin so we didn't change to that brand. Auntie Ethel, who had no children of her own, was also kind to me as a child and occasionally I would stay with her and my uncle. My aunt was an excellent baker and I always used to be allowed to lick the baking bowl clean when the bun cases were filled, yummy! My cousin Eileen lived at Carver Clough, near the Royal Hotel in Ripponden. She would come to play out with me in the mill yard opposite when I stayed at Auntie Ethel's. We used to climb into the large basket-type skips that were there. I had once gone to stay with Auntie Nellie and Uncle Alec (Mother's brother) at Carver Clough but after so many days decided that I had been there long enough and wanted to go home to Sowerby. So my aunt took me back home by bus. Mother was in the washhouse busy at the mangle and was not at all amused that I had come home before the arranged date. She was not very good at coping with the unplanned or unexpected so my reception was "cool". But I knew that home was where I wanted to be.

Below the Almshouses at number 1, Town Gate, lived Mr Owen and Mrs Elsie Pickles and their daughter Audrey, who was born in 1921. Mr Pickles was a painter and decorator and had men working for him. They were friends of our family and I remember Mrs Pickles, a small lady, and her husband, usually in his white overalls. There were four houses in the block when Audrey lived there.

Next door lived Mrs Kitchen and at the rear sisters Barbara and Edith Crossley, then came a Mrs Scratchard. Later I remember when Mr Pickles' sister Ethel lived round the back.

There used to be a few cottages on the bend leading onto Dean Lane where the grassed area now is. In the first one lived Mr and Mrs Ellis with their daughter Betty. Then Mr Kevern Thorpe and his wife Nora Ellen with their three children, Margaret, Billy and Geoffrey and next door to them lived Mr and Mrs Robinson. At the rear of the cottages there were gardens.

As a railway worker, Mr Thorpe wore navy blue working attire and a cap and he sometimes carried an enamel "Billy-can" type of container for holding a drink of tea. He used to keep pigeons and was once featured on a television advert for Rolos chocolates, made by Mackintosh's of Halifax. It was filmed at his pigeon loft in Sowerby New Road (the Plantation) and he was shown enjoying a Rolo while he waited for the return of his pigeons. The voice-over was done later at their home in Whiteley Avenue at Beechwood, where they had moved to live in the new housing estate. Margaret who now lives in Burnley explains that the advert was shown a few times on television. She said the family found the experience of being involved with the filming quite exciting at the time, although it didn't earn them much cash!

Mrs Thorpe was a sewer and did clothing alterations for our family, as mother wasn't handy with needle and thread. She would shorten items of clothing and put new zips into garments for our family.

In November 2006 I made email contact with Bill Thorpe who now lives in Melbourne, Australia. He was a newspaper boy in Beechwood and remembers taking 29 papers on his round, which started at Steep Lane then down the fields into Boulderclough, up Pinfold Lane to the Church Stile before finishing at Pollit Avenue. He was paid 2/8d a week but remembers the residents of Boulderclough being particularly generous with their tips at Christmas. Some winters he struggled through heavy snow to make sure all his customers had their papers.

Bill Heap and young neighbour Geoffrey Thorpe with the snowman & igloo he made.

Geoffrey, Bill's late brother, had a photograph taken outside St Peter's Church in the snow one winter and this was published in the *Evening Courier*. Bill thinks the family moved to Whiteley Avenue in the Beechwood estate around 1950 or '51 and he attended Rooley Lane Methodist Chapel for some years. He was a cornet player and, as well as taking part in Christmas shows for the Sunday School, he would play with Ryburn School Band, Sowerby Bridge Brass Band, Friendly Band and also made appearances with Black Dyke Mills Junior Band. For nineteen years he was in the St John's Ambulance, Sowerby Bridge Division, and before he left for Australia was the Area Cadet Officer for the West Riding of Yorkshire. Bill worked as a saw-maker at Dakin's in Friendly, Sowerby Bridge, leaving in 1977, when he became the first saw-maker to migrate to Australia. He retired at the age of 55 after running his own rubber moulding business. A keen ten-pin bowler, he met his wife Brenda at the former bowling alley in Broad Street (now Netto) in Halifax. The couple have been bowling ever since and have represented the state team of Victoria several times, also as seniors. When he sold his business he bought the factory and installed two bowling lanes and so his great passion for the game continues.

Another lady who helped with clothing alterations was Mrs Sutcliffe on the Newlands. Her son John worked and lived for many years as a butcher in South Africa. Recently I popped into the local Supermarket in Sowerby and spotted a familiar face – sure enough, it was John who now lives in Well Head Lane. We hadn't seen each other for well over 40 years! Terry, his brother, was a talented cartoonist and artist. Tragically, following an accident, he was confined to a wheelchair and used to live in a converted bungalow at Lower Bentley Royd.

Down on the farm

The farm was the place where my friends and I spent a great deal of time. From an early age animals have always been important to me and I feel privileged to have experienced a childhood that contained wonderful times surrounding the seasons of the farming routine. At Town Farm lived Mr James (Jimmy), Mrs Hannah Jane (Janie) and their son Dennis Greenwood who had been born at Pinfold Green before they moved up to Town Farm. The family also had Stile Farm just behind the Church Stile Inn. Jimmy was a local councillor on the old Sowerby Bridge Urban District Council. He would delight in grabbing hold of me when I was a small girl, as I peered into the dairy, to give me some "chin pie" and my fair skin would become reddened with his rough growth of stubble. He had quite a temper and not a lot of patience so it was not unusual to see him lose it and hear some choice words. He did soften later when Dennis married Marion Lumb at Scout Road Methodist Chapel, Mytholmroyd, on September 17th 1953. Dennis was a past chairman of Halifax Young Farmers' club and Marion was a past secretary of Hebden Bridge Young Farmers' club and things seemed to take on a calmer atmosphere with her presence. She used to ride up on her horse from Mytholmroyd when they were courting and she would tether it to the mistle door for the duration of her visit.

Pigs were reared and I used to love to go and see the new-born piglets. Sadly there was usually a dead one or one which the mother had squashed, also a "runt" which needed some extra feeding and caring for, and here the feeding bottle came into use. It was fun when the piglets were big enough to be let out of the sty to chase around and explore the yard. They used to come to my feet and undo my shoe laces with their little snouts. If a pig was due to farrow, then it was likely that someone would be up during the night to see that all went well with the birth. When the milk round was done, people would put out waste for the pigs to be made into swill and this would include cabbage leaves, other vegetable matter, stale bread, in fact anything suitable for the pigs to eat. Collections of food waste were also made at St Peter's School in Sowerby and at Sowerby Bridge Grammar School. Down the garage at the side of the farm where the milk truck used to park, there was a boiler which provided steam for the bottle cleansing in the dairy. When this job was completed the steam was used to heat up the swill in dustbins to feed the pigs. There was quite a smell when that was cooking up! The only problem with a visit to look at the pigs was the fear of seeing a rat; occasionally this happened and a hasty retreat was made, probably accompanied by a loud shriek or scream. When Colin Jowett, who worked for Greenwoods for many years, caught a rat in the large trap, he used to drown it in one of the baths at the farm that were full of water. Those rats were big creatures.

Colin (known as the Colonel) was quite a character. He had a loud voice which he once used to promote the Conservative party. He made a mistake when he tried to convert the Smiths next door when canvassing. They were red-hot Labour and after a heated discussion, Colin made a hasty retreat down the path and didn't call again. His father and mother, Donald and Clarinda (Linda), lived in a cottage in St Peter's Square, facing the school playground. Mr Jowett used to work for Thornbers at Mytholmroyd while Mrs Jowett was a dinner lady at St Peter's Infants School just over the wall. Mr Jowett was always in Wellington boots, he had a smallholding across the road below the church where he kept hens and ducks. Mr Tommy Cardwell from Pollit Avenue also kept a variety of livestock there. Bill Heap, his wife Annie, who died in July 2005, and sons Roger and John lived in the house next to the archway opposite the church, in St Peter's Square. This area was at one time a garrison for the Roundhead soldiers; some are supposed to be buried in the graveyard across the road. When Colin married in 1954, the newly-weds went to live in a rented cottage at Wood Lane off Pinfold Lane. Mr Edgar Lumb was the landlord and he charged them 7/6 a week rent. Colin's wife-to-be Sheila first saw the cottage from the Pollit Avenue bus stop when there was a deep snow and Colin asked if she fancied living there as it was available to rent. So they married soon after and went on to have three children: Richard, born 1955, Linda, born 1956, and Sharon, born 1964. Sheila had the steep Wood Lane to tackle when she went out and pushing a pram over that rough surface must have been very hard work. When she visited her mother in Siddal the pushchair would be left in the bull hole at Stile Farm and picked up on her return journey. Before her marriage Sheila had worked for Walker's department store in Northgate, Halifax, starting in the household department and moving onto the lingerie and underwear section. She then began to train as a corsetiere for Camp, who were specialists in the trade, with Mrs Marion Penny who was manageress of that department. They travelled to London when Sheila was eighteen to train with other ladies from various stores in other areas. Colin's first job was working for the GPO as a telegraph boy, and my brother David would often accompany him on his delivery round on the tops above Sowerby. He then worked for Saville Rowntree farming and went to Greenwoods when he was eighteen. He was exempt from doing his National Service as by then Jimmy Greenwood was ill, so Colin was needed on the farm and he stayed in that employment until he was about forty-two years old. He bred and showed sable rabbits and won many prizes and awards. Colin and Sheila also ran a kennels and cattery at Wood Lane called Mireywall Kennels. When Colin left farming he had several business ventures, including a butcher's shop in Elland, where Ian Cardwell worked with him. The marriage broke up in about 1976.

I can remember when the milking of the cows was done by hand, a long, slow and laborious job. Dennis or Colin would be seated on a small three-legged stool, their head pressed against the side of the beast, with a pail under the cow's udders to catch the milk. As youngsters we would watch this taking place, sometime to be squirted with milk from the teat, to our surprise! The pail was emptied into a large milk churn which, when full, would be rolled down the garage into the dairy. During winter months the cows remained in the mistal, just standing and sitting in the same spot. There were no exercise areas for the animals in those days; how tedious it must have been for them. No wonder when they were turned out in the springtime they would run and jump, rub their heads into the soil and delight in kicking it up over their backs. I have always enjoyed seeing the cows let out for their freedom in the fields and feel quite disappointed if I miss the event. The mistal in winter had a cosy feel to it; the atmosphere was steamy and the smell of manure and fodder mingled with the noises of the beasts eating their feed, buckets scraping on the stone floor. Then there was the slight hissing noise of them getting a drink of water from the metal bowls with a pad they pushed down with their noses. Sometimes we were allowed to help mix their food which was kept in a huge kist in the lathe. Dennis would have all the buckets lined up, measure the amount out with a scoop and we would give it all a stir with a stick. When a cow was feeling a bit "off colour", a dollop of black treacle or perhaps molasses was added to the mixture, to perk the beast up again.

To gain entry to watch the milking in the small mistal, I had to walk between two cows to get to where I could stand and watch. This at times took some considerable nerve as cows then used to have horns! (The odd one didn't and that was called a "Polly".) I used to try and gauge the best moment to pass between these big cows. Frightened that I would be squashed or kicked by them, I somehow used to make it through and feel relieved that I had! The arrival of a new calf was always enjoyed by us children especially when it needed to be taught to drink: we would put our fingers into a pail with some milk in and the calf would suck them and siphon up some milk at the same time. I have a great affection for cows. Some people class them as being stupid but they are not. Over the years I have witnessed many calves being born in the fields around us and I never cease to be moved by the sight of the cow dealing with its new baby, licking and cleaning it, gently mooing and tending it. Next the tentative staggering motions of the calf attempting to stand up for the first time and hopefully find the source of its food. Then usually with a bit of gentle shoving and nudging by the mother the udder is found! Occasionally the other cows may attempt to take over the new calf as they can be very nosey and curious animals.

The dairy was somewhere we children could also give a hand and we were often asked to help to put the tops on the milk bottles when a crate was full. The bottling machine was a simple contraption with a tank for the milk at the top. The bottles were then worked by handles to press them upwards so that the milk ran into them. The earlier tops were waxed and the bottle necks were wide, so it just required the tops to be pressed down into the neck. With the advent of TT milk in later years, the bottle tops were narrower and foil caps were placed on the top of the bottle and pressed down with a metal and rubber capper. Only occasionally were we allowed to use the bottling machine, usually sitting on an upturned milk crate to do the job. Then the truck and the van would be loaded up for the milk delivery. Colin used to wash and sterilise the returned empty milk bottles which in those days came in pint and half pint sizes. He spent a lot of time cleaning the bottles, wearing a big rubber apron and his Wellington boots. In the back of the dairy was a large walk-in fridge which always made me a little wary as it didn't have a handle on the inside. If I needed to go in the fridge for anything I always tried to make sure that the door was open as wide as possible – and get out of there as quickly as I could!

The milk round took in Sowerby village and the housing estates of Newlands, Newlands Avenue and Broadway up to Rooley Heights. Lower down the Beechwood estate would be covered and later the development at Brockwell. As children we used to help with the delivery but only when we had either Dennis or Marion's permission to do so. Riding in the back of the truck was great fun, sometimes on the tailgate which we shouldn't really have done. We helped put the milk onto the doorsteps and picked up the empties, not always very pleasant if the bottle hadn't seen any hot water and had a good rinse out. We also picked up the scraps for the pigs. The eggs were usually in the front of the truck and could be left as requested by the customer.

There were several hen cotes at the farm – in particular I remember a big one just beyond the pig styes on the field. There were also night arks down in the field over the wall from Church Terrace in Pinfold Lane. These had a slatted floor to let air in and were used to rear pullets. Collecting the eggs was fun apart from the little skin bites that I would sometimes get from hen lice, I suspect. To lift a new-laid warm egg out of a nesting box just vacated by the hen was lovely but cleaning them could be quite a different matter! This task was done down the garage in a little building next to an outside toilet. A bucket of water and some muslin cloth was needed to remove hen muck, congealed blood and anything else that was alien to a nice-looking free range egg. Colin had a quick method for dealing with some of the broken eggs, he would simply throw back his head and down his throat the raw egg slid! Another large hen hut was at the top of the Greenwoods' field which Mr Kerridge rented to keep poultry. It had once been the Sowerby band's rehearsal hut! The Kerridge sisters also had an allotment on land to the left of the top farm yard (over the wall from 36, Highfield Place). They spent many happy hours here over the years cultivating the land, growing vegetables and flowers. (The allotment is visible on the aerial view on p. 109, to the rear of the newly built house on Jack's hen pen.)

Down at Stile Farm or the "Bottom Shop" as it was known, the bull was kept, also Bob, the white cart horse. It was here that the Greenwoods had farmed before moving up to Town Farm. Outbuildings were used for cows in various stages of their growth. The barn was used to store hay and there were two milking sections. A few geese were kept down here and they were a bit nasty. They would come towards us with their necks outstretched and hissing and we used to retreat as fast as we could because a peck from those beaks would have hurt! The Church Stile Inn was run by Joe Coley and his wife Nellie and they had a son, Terry. They were the licensees at the pub from 1940 to 1957 and Mr Coley also worked for many years for Eglin Contract Furniture in Sowerby Bridge. He retired after serving 50 years with the firm and was tube shop manager for the last fifteen of these. By this time they had left the pub and lived in Pye Nest Road. Mr Milton Smith, our next door neighbour and the firm's longest serving employee, presented him with an electric lawn mower on behalf of the workers and the joint managing director Mr WE Collinson gave him a cheque on behalf of the firm. Mrs Coley later worked for many years as an assistant at Healey's coffee shop in George Square, Halifax.

We often used to find discarded bottle-tops in assorted colours behind the pub and we would fix them onto our blazer lapels, held in place by the bit of cardboard from inside the top. As children we visited Bob the all-white carthorse and took him treats of carrot, apple and sugar lumps. The yellow milk float was kept under a storage shed and it was here that Bob was harnessed up in the shafts and the milk, then in churns, was delivered around the village. It was measured out into milk jugs left on doorsteps or in window bottoms and a clean lace-edged cover was used to keep the flies out. Before we had milk from Greenwoods we used to have it delivered in this way by Stanley Barrett from Boulderclough. With the introduction of milking machinery the whole process became much quicker. The milk was still emptied into the churn and then taken to the dairy. Later the milk would be piped directly down there.

Dennis and the farm's first Limousin bull, Carthorpe Allan in Queen Street showing the Church Stile Inn, early 1980s. This picture appeared in a national newspaper.

Dennis would walk the bull up from the bottom farm (usually with someone else with him) to the top yard at Town Farm when the animal was required to serve a cow. This was always a fairly dangerous job always with the risk of something going wrong and the children were told to keep well out of the way when "Billy" was around the area. There was almost a tragedy involving the bull in October 1968 when Colin was pinned against the wall while attending to the animal in the building where he was kept. His son Richard heard him yell out so he grabbed a muck fork, dashed into the bull hole and jabbed the animal several times. His dad was pinned in a corner but he managed to scramble up and the bull got its head underneath him and pushed him upwards. There was now only the wood partition, about an inch thick, between the bull hole and safety. Richard dashed out, bolted the door and helped his father into the stable section. People from the nearby Church Stile Inn had heard the commotion and came out to see what was happening. Someone called for an ambulance and Colin was taken to the Halifax Royal Infirmary where he stayed for several days. The outcome could have been very serious as the bull was fully grown with horns. The vicar of Sowerby, the Rev WJ Gibson, visited Colin and, when he heard about Richard's bravery, he decided to write to "Blue Peter", the children's television programme, as he thought that his courageous act should be recognised properly with an award. Richard was presented with the Blue

Peter Gold Medal at Ryburn School in 1969 by the headmaster Mr RS Miles and the story was featured in the *Halifax Evening Courier*. Colin, who died in July 2002, went on to work at the farm for many years.

Colin Jowett on the new tractor, May 1960.

Haymaking was always a special time for the children because we were allowed to get involved and help out, along with the adults. Hopefully the weather would remain dry once the grass had been cut and then the process of turning it would take place. Mrs Greenwood made sandwiches and pots of tea, put them into a large basket and Pat Dixon and I would take it onto the workers in the field. There was a lot of physical work involved and helpers would come to assist both in the fields and at the farm, getting the hay up into the loft. The hay would be raked into lines and then into piles. Bob was used to pull the cart and the hay would be forked up onto the back of the cart with someone eventually sitting a-top a good pile of hay. This was then taken back along the fields to the barn where the cart would be backed in through the barn doors. Then there was the task of forking the hay up onto the first stage middle landing of the barn (with the arched window looking down to where I now live), then it had to be forked up into the main space to the left and to the right. This process went on until all Greenwoods' fields had been "housed". As the barn became fuller we children would trample the hay down so that more could be added. This was a hot and stuffy job to do and perspiration would drop from our foreheads. Eventually the barn would be full of sweet-smelling hay ready to feed the cattle in the winter months. The ladder into the loft was tied securely but it was vertical. I remember climbing it once behind Ian Cardwell who was home on leave from the forces and had come to help with the haymaking. I was a bit too close behind him and got struck on my forehead with one of his boots. The descent down the ladder was pretty swift and I ran up home crying. Mother was asking me what had happened when poor Ian came to the house to see how I was and to apologise for hurting me. Needless to say, after a few minutes I felt better and returned to the farm. That knock taught me to leave a bit of distance when climbing ladders behind someone, a valuable lesson.

The tractor, a grey Massey Ferguson, was also used at haymaking time. Fields were "housed" at Town Farm, down Pinfold Lane and down Littlewood Lane as far as the railway line. A treat at the end of the day would be a ride on Bob back to the farm. Colin or Dennis would hoist me up onto his broad back and I would feel very high indeed off the ground. Mother would give me strict orders about what time I had to be in at night especially if it was school the next day. On one occasion she had told me to be in for when the church clock struck nine, but on a beautiful evening in the haymaking fields when you are having a good time, somehow time is the last thing on your mind. Mother appeared, striding onto the field and was not amused as I had passed the time deadline. She strode out and ordered me to get on home and my gabardine belt that she had brought with her rattled around my legs all the way on home. When my mother said a certain time she meant it: she couldn't stand a lack of punctuality and was always on time.

Dennis and Marion's only child Susan was born on July 5th 1968; they had been married for married for eighteen years. Marion continued to work as normal on the farm until her baby was born. In later years Dennis purchased Littlewood Lane Farm and Barn hoping to eventually retire there. Sadly he died suddenly on May 11th 1995. The cattle were taken on by Norman Hitchen, Dennis's cousin up at Crib Farm, Luddenden Foot the following November. Marion and Susan moved to occupy the properties at Wood Lane during 1998. John Hitchen, Norman's son, bought Town Farm and raises cattle there.

Marion with Susan her daughter and James our son, on Harvey,
Wood Lane, July 1974.

In the autumn we would go blackberrying, each of us setting off with a two-pound jam jar for the railway embankment at the bottom of Wood Lane. This is where the largest, juiciest berries were to be found. The brambles down the lane had plenty of berries but the ones above the rail track were the best. Our jam jars soon filled up and we didn't mind the scratches from the brambles or the wasps that always seemed to buzzing around them. We always used to duck down when a train came along the line – it was after all railway property – and we thought perhaps we could get into trouble for trespassing. Some of the blackberries would be eaten while we were picking. But I was never too keen on that as I knew that when I got them home and put the berries to soak, after removing the stalks, quite a lot of tiny dead worms would come out of the fruit – and I didn't want those wrigglers in my tummy! The fruit would most likely be put into a crumble, perhaps with an addition of baking apples. There was a craze at one time for having a "ginger beer" plant. Someone would have passed on the base compound and this required feeding with sugar and ginger powder. After a certain time water was added to turn it into ginger beer. We would save up empty Ben Shaw's pop bottles from the fish shop and sieve the stuff off into them, and very good it tasted too! Another drink we would make was "Spanish water", which we would take with us on our picnics and adventures in the fields or along Dean Lane into the bluebell woods. Following the stream we would walk through Gracie Fields (grazing fields) where forget-me-nots, milkmaids and harebells grew along the stream. It was also a great source of frogspawn which we collected in jam jars and took home. I kept mine on the inside of the washhouse window bottom and waited for it to develop into tadpoles, which were then given fine breadcrumbs to eat. It was great to watch them develop, get bigger and grow legs. When they reached a certain stage it was time to let them go as we didn't want to be overrun with the creatures so it was either back to the stream or maybe a trip down to the Finkle Dam to set them free.

Fun and games

There were many things to do when playing out with friends when we were youngsters. The summers always seemed to be long and hot and we took our jam sandwiches and bottles of water into the fields, enjoying picnics up on Rooley fields and the Delf. These fields were later spoiled when houses and flats were built on them. During the warm weather the clothes horse (winter hedge) would be taken when not in use into the back yard to be made into a tent – rather difficult because it was a three-sectioned clothes horse! I think we discovered that it was best used up against a wall so it had a roof and a side, and the third section was on the ground. With an old blanket spread out on the grass and some old curtains or covers over the frame, a sort of tent-cum-den was made. Into this small space one or two of us could squeeze to read comics, books or play with Snap cards. No doubt the cat would join us in the tent.

Pat, Terry and me, about 1948.

The flags were often chalked up for a game of hopscotch or we would play whip and top. I had a good selection of tops in differing shapes and sizes, which I kept in an old shoe box in one of the bottom cupboards in the living room. I would clean the old chalk off the tops and make new patterns and rings of different chalk colours. The whip was a piece of thin leather strip fastened onto a small stick. The tail was then wrapped around the top and the idea was to get it spinning by letting it go on the flags, then to keep it spinning by whipping it. This could go on for some time with practice and the chalked colours looked like a rainbow as the top spun round. On wet days we used to play in David's bedroom, Dixons' wash house or in Hartley's garage which was in the bottom corner of our back yard, when the black Ford Prefect Mr Hartley owned was not in there. In the bottom cupboard at home there was a black tin helmet with an old piece of elastic under the chin and the initials ARP on it. This stood for Air Raid Protection; as a child I didn't wear it, but liked to put it on the floor, sit in it and spin round and round – great fun! Skipping was popular and if we had a big rope out and someone to turn at each end, then perhaps we would play at "soldiers", running through and then increasing our jumps in the rope for as long as we could before we eventually trod on it and were declared "out". We played skipping games with accompanying rhymes; one of them went something like the following – (adapted version) "I know a little boy and he's double jointed, I gave him a kiss and made him disappointed, I gave him another to match the other, by gum Jean Smith I'll tell your mother for kissing Tony Wilson down by the river, how many kisses did you give the little fellow?" The rope was then turned faster and the "kisses" counted until the person skipping trod on the rope and was "out". School playgrounds were popular for skipping games and I remember sometimes it was difficult to judge the right time to run and get into the rope and start jumping and my head would be going in motion with the rope turns until I made the move. Dipping was used to establish who was to be "in" or "it" before the start of a game. One verse was "There's a party on the hill, will you come? Bring your own cup and saucer and a bun. What colour dress will you wear? R-E-D spells red and O-U-T spells out." Then another was "Dip dip dip, my blue ship, sailing on the water like a cup and saucer, dip dip dip, you do not have it". A short one went "Little boy scout walk out" or "One potato, two potato, three potato, four, five potato, six potato, seven potato, more". Done with our clenched fists, if you had "more" on your fist, it went behind your back, and so on until one person was left "in". If a child was thought to be telling lies or "fibbing", as we called it, we would say, "Tell tale tit, your tongue will split and all the cats and dogs will have a little bit". "Ring a ring a roses, a pocket full of posies, atishoo, atishoo, we all fall down" was done by joining hands and skipping around. "Oranges and lemons" was, I think, two people making an archway with their upstretched hands and people passing through and being "caught" when their hands came down. "Skitter scatter" was when two people crossed wrists and joined hands with toes touching. They would lean back and spin faster and faster until they became too dizzy and had to stop. We used to play at "Donkey" where a few of us would line up, throw the ball at the wall and take turns to jump over it. Ball games were always popular and stumps would be chalked on the wall for games of cricket; we also played at rounders. Boys and girls played marbles and I was popular in this game as I had acquired most of my brother David's collection of assorted glassies, in all sizes and colours, including some blood "ollys" in red and white. There were also some chalky white ones which were used in the game of Knur and Spell and silver ball-bearings of assorted sizes. Mine were kept in a white drawstring bag and we loved to collect and swap our marbles.

In autumn we collected conkers from the horse chestnut trees, probably on Dean Lane. These would be soaked in vinegar to harden them and make them stronger for conker fights. There would have to be some help from an adult with putting the string through the conker and tying off with a knot. The winner was the child with the toughest conker to survive all the hits – and the toughest knuckles to survive all the mis-hits. "Knock and Run" was often played by us children, much to the consternation of the unfortunate resident who had been disturbed from their armchair to answer the door to find no-one there. We would be hidden round a corner sniggering at the plight of the person who was by now peering up and down the street, realising they had been had again. One time we knocked on Terry's Auntie Clarice's door and, when she spotted us, I remember she called out to me, "You're just as bad as the lads, Jean Smith" and, of course, I was. Another game was "Tracking" which involved someone designated the finder and the others given some time to get as far away as possible, leaving arrows chalked onto the flags or walls to indicate the route taken. Then the finder would seek the others, who by now were hidden and trying to keep quiet, by following the arrows. It seems a bit tame when you describe the game now, but we used to enjoy playing it.

My brother's bicycle was passed down to me when I was tall enough to pedal it. So I became the proud owner of a green, full-size, gent's Raleigh bike with saddle-bag and drop handlebars. It also had toe clips, which could be a bit awkward if you were about to fall off the machine, as you needed to get your toes out of the clips rather quickly. When I had given it a clean with Duraglit and polished it off with a soft cloth, that bike and its chrome spokes shone and glinted in the sunshine. Many happy hours were spent on that bike. I remember first becoming aware of the latest music, rock and roll, as I rode past John and Derek Higgins' house on the Newlands and hearing "Bye Bye Love" by the Everly Brothers blaring out from their record player on the front porch. Malan Ford and I used to cycle to the rec. at Ripponden, to meet up with Tony Brunning who was known as "Bunney" and other friends, to laugh and chat as youngsters do. The longest trip that Malan and I made was to Farsley near Pudsey to see two workmen, electricians called Norman and Colin. They were still working on the new Ryburn School when we moved up there from Sowerby New Road Secondary Modern School, after it merged with the boys from Bolton Brow School in February 1959. We became friendly with them and they once visited us to have tea at our house. Malan and I recklessly decided to ride over and visit them and almost completed the bicycle journey when we got cold feet near Farsley and headed home again!

Soon after the month of September was out, we children would start our preparations for our bonfire or "Plot" as it was also called. We used to go plotting in earnest and collections of household rubbish and anything suitable for burning would be accepted. Places of storage included the Dixons' washhouse, the Hartleys' shed and our back yard. Things had to be guarded and stored somewhere safe as raids by rival gangs were commonplace and a lot of our hard work could be wiped out in one fell swoop. We would trail round the village with an old bogey to pile the junk in, knocking on doors and begging for rubbish. We accumulated a lot of junk from Dennis's farm and Plot Night gave him the opportunity to have a good clear out. Old papers and books were not collected until nearer the date as they became damp in storage. We held the bonfire in the field at the rear of The Royd, building it on a flat piece of ground more or less opposite Alec Smith's joinery shop. It took quite some time and physical effort for us to drag all our stuff on there. I think Dennis probably gave a hand here with his tractor and trailer. We were always glad if we were given an old chair or settee to burn – it was usually kept for people watching the bonfire to sit on until it was time to add it to the flames and watch it burn. There was also a homemade "Guy" of sorts to put on top of the bonfire, decked out in old clothes and with a cap and scarf added to his outfit. In the weeks leading up to November 5, I would begin my collection of fireworks as soon as I had any money to spare. The fireworks were kept in a glass display case at Sowerby Post Office and I used to love looking at the selection available and planning which ones to buy with my coppers. There would be Roman candles, which shot out different coloured balls at intervals, chrysanthemum fountains, snowstorms and Catherine wheels of assorted sizes. The favourite for little children were Sparklers which would be circled round in a gloved hand, making patterns in the night air. Rockets would be set off from a jam jar and we always wondered where the stick would land! There were jumping crackers large and small, and bangers called Little Demon and the louder Cannon – I wasn't too keen on these as the lads used to enjoy throwing them. We could buy boxes of fireworks made by Standard of Huddersfield and Lyon. They would vary in price but if you had one for 2/6 that was good and if you had one for 5 shillings, that was even better. My brother worked at one time for WH Smith in Halifax at their warehouse on Union Street and he once brought me some indoor fireworks home to try but they made such a lot of smoke and smelt so terrible that we didn't try them again. One Bonfire Night Mother and I went up to my Uncle Jack's, Auntie Melinda's and twelve cousins at Field End Farm, Triangle. They had built a huge plot in the road up to the farm and all our fireworks were put into a shopping bag but not long after the fire was lit, a spark got into the bag and within seconds the whole lot went up with assorted flashes and bangs. Our display ended very quickly, something of an anti-climax to the night!

We always kept our fingers crossed for fine weather in early November and the final building and stacking of the pile would take up a lot of our time that day if it fell on a Saturday. There was usually a good turn out of people to watch the fireworks and enjoy the fire and lots of similar bonfires would be visible right across the valley. As the fire burned and the heat increased, we had to move back where it was cooler. An assortment of food would be provided by parents, parkin, Plot toffee and potatoes baked in the hot embers and covered in melted butter – no potatoes tasted better than these! Maybe a few chestnuts would be added to the fire for us to sample. We all shared and enjoyed the show of fireworks together and a good time was had by everyone. It was usually a late bed night as the fire would last a long time and eventually the settee or the old chair was thrown on to make it burn for a bit longer. The following morning we would trail onto the field to rake the glowing embers and try to rekindle a flame as we picked up and disposed of the empty fireworks containers, and always made sure that the field was left neat and tidy. Bonfires have now become more organised and fireworks are used to celebrate special occasions throughout the year, not only November 5. Many spectacular displays have been viewed from our sitting-room window across the valley. The Millennium celebrations across Calderdale were stunning and went on for what seemed an eternity. Next morning the pall of low cloud, the aftermath of all the fireworks, took several hours to clear.

Another favourite source of amusement was the radio, or wireless as we called it. I loved "Journey into Space", with its haunting introductory theme music, "Dick Barton", the special agent with his assistant Snowy, the Paul Temple series of detective mysteries, "Educating Archie" with Peter Brough and his dummy – how strange to have a ventriloquist on the radio when you think about it! During lunchtime there was "Workers' Playtime", broadcast from workplaces and factories in various parts of the country. I remember Anne Shelton as one of the singers and Charlie Chester made us laugh with his jokes. "Listen with Mother" was at 1.45pm; I can hear the signature tune in my head to this day! We used to listen to this broadcast from a big Bakelite radio at St Peter's Infant School every day. There were little songs to sing along with, followed by a story. When we were very young this was perhaps followed by a lie-down on a mat and even a short nap. "Mrs Dale's Diary" followed later in the afternoon and she always seemed to be "worried about Jim", her husband. I remember "Life with the Lyons" featuring Ben Lyon, his wife Bebe, their children Richard and Barbara and their home helper Aggie, played by Mollie Weir. "The Clitheroe Kid" was broadcast from 1958 to 1972 and starred the comedian Jimmy Clitheroe with his Mum, Granddad and sister Susan, known as "scraggy neck". Tony Hancock and Sid James in "Hancock's Half Hour" and "The Goons" were enjoyed but Mother couldn't stand "The Billy Cotton Band Show" on Sundays. As soon as he shouted "Wakey Wakey!" the radio went off. We did listen to "Family Favourites", hosted by husband and wife team Cliff Michelmore and Jean Metcalfe. They presented a two-way request programme for people serving in the forces, usually linking up with Germany and sometimes Cyprus. Mother liked to listen to the pianist Semprini who used to introduce his programme "Semprini Serenade" of beautiful melodies, old ones, new ones, loved ones and neglected ones. Another of her favourites was "Grand Hotel" on Sunday nights, which had the Palm Court Orchestra playing classical music and rousing overtures. Mother loved this sort of music and also brass band tunes. She had once conducted a brass band in Happy Valley in Llandudno when I was young and we were there on holiday. At one point in her life she had been brought up by a great uncle who had taught her to appreciate good music. Another radio favourite was "A Life of Bliss" with George Cole; there was a dog called Psyche with the voice of Percy Edwards, the man with a gift for animal impersonations on the radio and later on the television. "Have a Go" was hosted by Halifax-born Wilfred Pickles and his wife Mabel. They travelled around to different towns with their quiz show and the chance to win cash, usually handed over with the words "Give him (or her) the money, Barney", Barney being the assistant on the show.

Two Penn'orth of Chips

Jack Wilcock, about 1987.

The local fish and chip shop, just below Providence Chapel, was owned by Jack Wilcock (real name John), who was a bit of a character in the village. He kept his hens in a large pen up the road next to Dixons' yard. It had two gated entrances and a few stone buildings where Jack kept an assortment of livestock, hens, ducks, rabbits and even a horse at one time. He had a collection of tools of every description for any job that cropped up and was always busy, dressed in his overalls, blue cotton jacket and Wellington boots. He was helped in the fish shop by his daughter Nois and daughter-in-law Mary who was married to his son Jack. They were quite different. Nois, with her beautiful peroxide blonde hair, always seemed very glamorous to me as a child. She had been in the forces (WAAF) and married a man called Wasil Bisofsky, a Bulgarian who at one time lodged with Arthur Jakeways in Beechwood. Wasil could not return to the country of his birth and he never saw his parents again. They had two children, Martin and Julie. By contrast, Mary was a more homely type, I thought, and also had two children, Michael and Lesley. Jack Wilcock was born in October 1901 and was married to Sarah Ann, who was always called Molly. They had three children, Jack the eldest, then Nois, and Dina, who married George Willey when he came to Soyland to farm from Preston. After moving from Allen Wood, Sowerby Bridge, they came to live at Richmond Gardens in Beechwood. On Wednesdays the fish shop closed and Jack and his wife would go to Halifax to have a meal out and visit the cinema to see a film. He never left his wife in the house alone: there was always someone to keep her company.

Sowerby Bridge Farmers' Association in the 1930s.

On the weekly night of the Sowerby Bridge Farmers' Association meetings, Lesley would sit in with her grandma until grandad returned. The housework was done by the daughters. The shop had a back place where Jack made his chips from potatoes that were kept in a large dolly-tub filled with water. It was dark and gloomy in there and the floor was uneven with gullies for the water to run away. The fish frying range was a yellow one, made by local firm Frank Ford. The quart bottles of Ben Shaw's pop were kept in the window bottom. Favourite flavours were dandelion and burdock, American cream soda (used also to make a drink with the addition of a scoop of ice-cream on a hot day), ginger beer, lemonade and orangeade. The children christened the shop "Jack's slug hole" because of the odd black offering and sometimes pallid state of the chips. The batter on the fish wasn't always crisp enough either so it was a question of getting your timing right and hoping for the best. As I queued in the shop for my order, shifting round as people were served, I would be trying to remember what I had to ask for but there was also something else on my mind. As I handed over my money to pay for the newspaper parcel, I would ask, "Have you any comics or magazines please?" Jack would peer over the counter at me and, if he had time, disappear round the back to sort me something out. These could be perhaps a *Girls' Crystal*, an *Eagle* comic which was more of a boy's read, sometimes there was an American comic included which was a bit of a treat. The odd *Photo Play*, *Titbits* or a copy of the *Reveille* was always welcome. I would leave the shop feeling pleased, not only because there going to be the chance of chips and even some fish, but also because I was anticipating sitting on the little buffet, up close to the fire for a good read of the papers and comics that Jack had given me. We used to collect our newspapers and send them down to the shop to be used for wrapping the fish and chips.

Jack's daughter Mary worked for a time for Jimmy Greenwood at Town Farm, helping with bottling of the milk. She also worked for more than thirty years at Eglin's furniture-makers in Sowerby Bridge. Lesley used to go in at school holiday time and help with the assembling of the flat pack TV stands. My mother also worked for Mr Wilcock, serving on behind the counter for a time when I was young. Kathleen Bohen, a friend of ours who was seven years older than me, used to look after me while she worked in the evenings. At a pre-arranged time she would bring me into the house from playing outside and supervise my getting washed and ready for bed, more difficult during the light nights I should imagine. Kathleen sometimes used to hoist me aloft to swing on the iron bars that protruded from the gas lamps near our house. As children we all used to congregate and play around the gas lamps. The last lamp lighter in Sowerby village was a Mr Shaw who lived in Sowerby New Road.

The fish shop moved down into the new row of shops built where the Rawson Almshouses stood. The block consisted of the fish shop, a wool shop, the Post Office run by Selwyn and Betty Hunt, Bob Steadman's greengrocers, a ladies' hairdresser's and Leslie Nicholls' newsagents. Jack had a fall off the roof of one of the buildings in his hen-pen and finished work shortly afterwards so Nois took over the running of the fish and chip shop. Later, visiting Dinah at Preston, Jack was taken ill with a heart problem and finally went into a home, where he wasn't happy and missed his home and the village of Sowerby. He died in May 1997 and Sowerby lost one of its most popular characters.

Rawson Almshouses, demolished in the 1950s.

The row of shops built in place of the almshouses. This photo was taken at 2pm on a Saturday, July 2003!

The Bohen family lived at 46, The Royd. Their house was the bottom one and was set back from the front of the building. When they first lived there it had an outside "tub" toilet with two holes in the wooden seat. This was later up-dated to a water-flushing lavatory but I do remember the pieces of newspaper fastened onto string on the back of the door, as there was no toilet roll. They kept a few hens in their back yard. The Bohens' door was never locked and visitors just walked into the passage and then into the living room with its black-leaded range. There was usually a blackened copper kettle simmering on the fire, ready to scald a pot of tea. Mrs Bohen's cheese and onion pasties were baked in the side oven of the range. It was a long room with one window overlooking the hen pen and one at the rear of the room with a deep window bottom. The house was under-built and, from the window at the rear, you could see the feet and legs of anyone walking down the footpath which led into Greenwood's field. The lighting was by gas and I remember the slight hissing noise that was emitted from the mantle – these were delicate and had to be handled with care as they soon damaged. There were beams in the living room and many times I was picked up by my elbows by either Peter, Kathleen's older brother, or maybe his friend Gerard Lynch, and raised up towards the beams to touch them with my head. As Mrs Bohen's health deteriorated, she moved into a single bed downstairs. Dr McKelvey was a regular caller and she used to have big bottles of medicine to take. The kitchen had a stone sink with a cold tap and a small window where the cat came in and out, and nothing much else. I was endlessly teased about the cat and told stories of how it wore little Wellington boots and a small raincoat to go outside – they told me with such conviction that I almost believed their tales. Up a rickety wooden staircase there were two adjoining bedrooms. Rosemary, the older sister, had lived at one time in Coventry but when she returned to Sowerby with her two little girls, one a toddler and one a baby, they stayed at number 46 and the baby slept in a deep drawer taken out of the sideboard. It was while sitting around the fire at the Bohens that I used to listen to all sorts of gossip and tales when I was a little girl. It was also here that I probably had my first attempt at puffing on a cigarette, as most of the household were smokers. There was always a packet of Capstan Full Strength and a big pint pot of strong sweet tea on the go.

I talked to Peter Bohen in 2006 at his flat in Hanson Lane, Halifax.

Peter worked in Halifax and Sowerby Bridge as a traffic warden in later years. It seems ironic that Peter now lives in sheltered housing where every door is locked for security reasons, and gaining admission is complex, as the house door at 46, The Royd was never locked day or night!

There were three children in the Bohen household, Rosemary, the eldest, born in 1932, then Peter, born in 1936, and the youngest Kathleen, born in 1937. There was never a Mr Bohen around in all the time I knew the family. Peter had rheumatic fever twice as a child, in 1939 when he was three years old and also in 1944 when he was seven. He had the misfortune to be thrown into the well opposite St Peter's Church by a group of evacuee children and became seriously ill. It took him twelve months each time to recover from the illness, an acute inflammatory disease of the lining and valves of the heart and larger joints, causing aching and pain. There was no hospitalisation for Peter and he was visited by Dr McKelvey at least once or twice a day to have medicine administered. Around the same time other children in the Sowerby area were struck down with rheumatic fever including Marion Gill, June Molly and Audrey Moore. During his recovery Peter had no schooling so he read anything and everything that he could lay his hands on to educate himself. These included all types of books, biographies, magazines and newspapers. When I was a toddler Peter would take me for walks in my pushchair, which had two wheels and a long handle to push it along. Rosemary used to tell the tale of how Peter was pushing me along in Sowerby Bridge in front of the Bull's Head pub when I fell out of the pram onto the hard cobbles. Fortunately no damage done, I was returned to the pram and we continued on our walk!

Peter started at St Peter's Infants School on his fifth birthday in April 1941. Mr Frank Fielding Hollas was then the headmaster and the teachers were Miss Edwin, Miss Taylor and Mrs Crossley who taught the basic three Rs, of reading, writing and arithmetic. The children played in the air raid shelters pretending to be soldiers and stole the strawberries which had been grown on top of the shelter by the headmaster. Peter went on to Bolton Brow Secondary School and doesn't remember sitting an 11-plus examination, possibly because of his absenteeism due to illness. When Peter was about eight years old he used to help my father with the movement of cattle up on the tops around Salt Pie Farm (my father sold this to Mr Arthur King). He remembers being taken into the Travellers' Rest at Steep Lane and given a gill of beer to drink and a cigarette to smoke. My father came to the rescue when Peter was struck in the eye by a pick-axe wielded by a lad digging in a yard across from The Royd. My father took him along to the hospital for treatment but, as a result of the blow, Peter's eyesight was permanently impaired.

Peter was a helper at Greenwoods at Town Farm from about the age of eight or nine. He collected hen eggs and was paid 2/6 a week and he also helped at hay-making time. For many years he was a friend of Colin Jowett and he remembers socialising and the good times they had together. He told me that Colin used to do public speaking at one time. I would have loved to have been at one of his venues to hear him speak – I know from personal experience that forty minutes takes some filling but Colin would have had no difficulty whatsoever in doing that!

Noises in the night and strange goings on

Sowerby Post Office and Mrs Georgeson's cottage next door below, the Smithy above and Nos. 57, and 59, Town Gate, the "haunted house" higher up the road.

During the mid-1950s my departure from the Bohens' house on dark nights was rather scary. This was due to the "going ons" at number 59, Town Gate, opposite the top of the Royd. The house had become newsworthy because of the presence of a poltergeist, which had been reported as "The Sowerby Ghost – Sowerby Mystery – The home where they dare not sleep". The couple who lived there were Doreen Georgeson and her husband Bogdan Tarandzief, who was Polish. They had moved from 53, Town Gate into number 59 when they married. The following report from a newspaper (probably the *Halifax Evening Courier*, as it was a local story, although I remember my aunt in Keighley telling my mother that the story had been reported in her local paper) was given to me by Herbert Smithson. It was undated and was a rather poor photocopy of the report so I struggled to read some of the details but it is interesting to note the style of reporting that was used at that time.

The report said: "They get home between five and six pm, have tea then sit in the living room for a couple of hours, have supper then leave for the night, his wife goes to her parents for the night. 'We have to do it – we just cannot sleep here,' she says. Mr Bogdan Taradzief sleeps in Halifax paying 15 shillings a week for his lodgings. Somewhere in the valley a clock chimed the half hour past eight. Time for the mill worker and his wife to leave their house for the night. Time for the father to dandle his little daughter on his knee and kiss her goodnight. Time for him to go back to his lodgings. 'You see we just cannot live here anymore,' said Bogdan. 'We haven't had a full night's sleep since October.' He is the tenant of 59, Town Gate, Sowerby, a neatly furnished little old house, one of two perched on the hill. He has lived there with his wife for nearly (illegible) years now, but they don't sleep there any more. 'And we won't until things are better,' he said. His wife, the former Miss Doreen Georgeson, took up the story; up to her marriage she lived with her parents, Mr and Mrs Gordon Georgeson at 53, Town gate, just a few yards down the lane.

"Noises in the Night: 'I'd heard stories before my marriage about the odd noise up the road in the night,' she said to a reporter. 'But when we got the chance of No. 59, we took it. It wasn't bad at first, and it was the first home of our own, we were determined to like it. Noises wakened us in the night; gradually it became just too bad for us to carry on. Both of us are working, we could not sleep, we had to go. There were terrible "rushing" noises, the jangling of pots in the kitchen early in the morning. Banging noises from the small back bedroom. We found doors opening after they had been fastened and when we went to look there was no one there. We never saw anything. One night we sat up in the living room stoking up the fire so that it was very warm. At 1am Lassie our dog whimpered suddenly. Then she scuttled back under the sofa, terrified.' The room was suddenly icy cold, they could not sleep. So Mrs Tarandzief went back to her old home to spend the nights with her parents, who were already looking after her baby Kateryna, 18 months old.

"Dog Terrified: Mr Gordon Georgeson took up the story. 'We haven't room for Bogdan here," he said. 'So he sleeps in lodgings in Halifax, goes to work in a mill at Shelf, then travels back to his home to spend the evening, every night he catches a late bus back to his lodgings. Once recently I went into number 59 when Bogdan and his wife had left for the night. I took Lassie with me, suddenly she leaped and whined in terrible fright. I saw a sudden glow, a glow of golden light coming apparently from down the bedroom stairs. At other times I have been told of lights in the house in the early hours but no-one was sleeping there, and so far as I know there was no-one in the house.'

"Next door at number 57 live Mr Herbert and Mrs Mary Smithson with their three children, Winifred, George and Susan. Mrs Smithson said, 'We have heard strange noises from next door for a long time, I thought Bogdan and Doreen must be moving the beds about or making furniture or something. It got so bad I decided to complain to them. The noises have gone on since they decided to sleep somewhere else, sometimes there are banging noises and the jangling of pots at one o'clock in the morning.'

"No reasonable explanation: What is the Cause? The wind? The tenants of both 57 and 59 say they have heard the noises on calm, windless nights. A practical joker? 'I thought of that,' said Mrs Smithson, 'but after all this time …?' Some odd Structural Defect? 'But what about the pots, the opening of doors that have been fastened?' asked Mrs Tarandzief. So far no-one has put forward a reasonable explanation, so every night a man and his wife have supper together, then the man walks round to his parents-in-law and kisses his daughter goodnight and the family is parted until the next evening."

The extraordinary events at the house led to Mr Quain, the electrician who had a shop on Wharf Street, Sowerby Bridge being called into help. Because he was a water diviner it was thought that perhaps he could help to cure or solve the problems in the house. Spending a night in the property with Peter Bohen and Colin Jowett for company, he used his hazel twig to test out the room and reported that he and Peter were dragged towards the house's party wall with the Smithsons. Scientists from Keighley came to investigate the haunting, which would explain the report in the Keighley newspaper. Their conclusion was that the presence in the house was Bogdan's mother and she was trying to contact him, causing all the disturbances. Another more local theory was that perhaps the family wanted to jump the council housing list and get a council house quicker. Unfortunately the unrest in the house continued and the two properties were vacated and demolished. When I used to leave the Bohens' house in the dark to go home, I would say my goodbyes, walk up the yard and find myself directly opposite the two empty houses, give them a furtive glance and then run like the wind, past the radio relay house, past the Post Office and its spooky porch, past the gateway into Jack Wilcock's hen pen, and then the dash to reach the doorway of 32, Town Gate, the only light in the street from the two gas lamps. Reaching home I would be out of breath but glad to be inside and safe. The ghostly stories stayed in my head for some time!

In the bleak midwinter . . .

Blizzard conditions in Pinfold Lane in the late '80s.

Winters could be long and heavy snowfalls were experienced during my childhood. I do not remember the deep snows of 1947 as I was only three years old but I know that it was a severe one. At the first warning of imminent snows, my Mother's first job was to make sure that the large shovel was brought into the house from the washhouse. This would most likely be needed to dig our way out in the morning as the snow had a tendency to drift up against our door. We used to get so much snow that walking on wall tops was not unusual. The snowfalls would sometimes last for days and this was the time we children loved – out came the sledges and candle-wax was rubbed onto the irons to make them go faster. Dressed in warm clothing and Wellington boots, we were ready for fun and games in Greenwoods' fields or whizzing down Queen Street, turning left into Pinfold Lane and speeding a long way down the hill. With little or no traffic in those days it was quite safe for us.

We would also sledge there at night-time under clear starlit skies when the surface would become smooth and glassy. We kept our fingers crossed that Tommy Cardwell and his crew in the council wagon didn't scatter ashes over the road surface in the morning and spoil our fun. Daytime sledging was usually in the fields and the one we used the most was the one with the footpath that came out into Row Lane. This field was steep and the speed would build up as you went downhill. This was not a "belly flat" field for me as it took a considerable effort to stop at the bottom of the field unless you decided to "bail out" before your feet thumped against the wall. The lads were a bit braver and would risk the "belly flat" position but care had to be taken as it was easy to whizz over the wall at the bottom.

Snow, sledges and smiles! (Approx 1950.) Taken in Mr Kerridge's field (rented from the farm) – the large hut at the rear is where the Old Sowerby Band used to practise. Left to right, Pat Dixon, Myself, Stuart Hartley, Terry Dixon and John Kerridge (to rear of sledge) and David Hartley.

We usually returned home wet and soggy but happy, snow down tops of boots, toes numb, gloves wet, fingers pinched, noses red, to thaw out in front of the fire with a cup of Bovril. Clothing was laid out on the hearth to dry for hopefully another sledging session the next day. We made slides and had a great time showing off our skills and styles while hoping to keep upright! We would start a snowball and soon it became quite large, needing two or three of us children to summon up our strength and push it until we could move it no further. The huge snowball would be left against a wall and lasted for days on end in the cold weather. Poor Geoffrey the butcher didn't appreciate our naughty ways when more than once a snowball would be thrown into the butcher's shop as the door opened. He would give us a good telling off, if we were still in sight, that is – usually we would have run off and be hidden safely round a corner. For some reason at the first fall of snow I always filled an enamel bowl with the new snow, brought it into the house and left it there overnight. When I got up in the morning the snow had melted and the bowl was, naturally, full of water. Why I wanted to do this is a mystery but the habit continued for several years. The buses used to struggle up Sowerby New Road through the snow. Ashes and cinders were kept under the steps to the upper deck and, if the bus was having trouble getting a grip, the conductor would be out with the shovel scattering ashes under the wheels – this usually worked. Even so, getting up as far as the end of the Newlands opposite the Co-op was sometimes as far as the buses could go, and Steep Lane and Hubberton would be a walking job but people just got on with it. Many hillside farmers and dwellers could be cut off for days in winter but schools didn't close and things didn't grind to a halt, life continued. One had to take care when the snow began to thaw and soften as huge and heavy lumps would shift and slide off the rooftops. There would be an almighty thud as the snow landed on the footpath under the windows at number 32. This snow was hard-packed and solid and even when thawing took days to melt and shift. The spectacular drifts and deep snows of my childhood no longer occur due to global warming. Even the smallest fall seems to create chaos these days and sadly the youngsters of today miss out on the fun of sledging and playing in the snow.

Chapel days

As soon as I was old enough to go to Sunday school, I began to attend the Congregational Chapel or "Old Green" as it was known, situated at the junction of Dob Lane and Well Head Lane above the Star Inn (now the Rushcart).

Sowerby United Reformed Church before demolition in 1980. Its original name had been Sowerby Congregational Chapel (known as "Old Green").

My brother David already attended there and we were both recorded with our dates of birth on the cradle roll that hung in the Primary there. The Sunday school was underneath the chapel, a huge impressive Gothic building which was to feature in my childhood for many years. On Sundays I would leave home early for the two o'clock service, as I liked to arrive before anyone else. As I walked up Town Gate the chapel was visible further up the road, with its imposing spire, large rose window and steps leading up to the main entrance through the gate and the graveyard. This was the way we would go in if it was a special service like the anniversary or the Harvest Festival. To go into normal Sunday school services, I went through the gate entrance on Dob Lane with the well in the wall next to it. The door would be open, and passing the boiler house there was usually a smell of sulphur in the air. I walked straight past the rows of empty wooden bench pews and headed for the piano at the front of the room; this would be played for our hymn singing when the service began later. The stage was at this end of the room and beyond that was the primary classroom and the kitchen. Sitting at the piano, I really wished that I could play the instrument properly, for music was not my strongest subject and learning to read music and understanding notes was not my greatest talent. I was just about able to play "The Lord is my Shepherd" with one hand or "Chopsticks" but I enjoyed sitting alone in this empty Sunday school gently trying to interpret some of the tunes from the hymn book that was propped up ready for use in the service. As people began to arrive I slid off the stool and sat on either the chairs for primary pupils or later the bench for older pupils. The vicar I remember was the Reverend R Handyside and I was friendly with his daughter Ruth, who was several years older than me. She had long dark hair in plaits. The family lived at the Manse, built in 1824, in Well Head Lane. If I remember correctly, there were periods of time when the chapel was without a vicar, or we would have visiting ones to do the preaching at times.

In later years the Manse was put onto the market, and after being empty for some time, was bought by Mr Colin Greenwood, his father Lloyd and mother Dorothy in December 1958. They had lived at Warley village where Mr Lloyd Greenwood had been sub-postmaster and also his father before him. They moved to Sowerby when they sold the business. The house had been used as a school during the mid-Victorian period, with the schoolroom situated to the left of the front door. When redecoration was carried out, it was possible to see the plaster where bench-type seating had been all around the four walls of the room. The mother of a Mr FW Teal walked from Lighthazels over the tops of Sowerby to be taught by the vicar of the time. Mr Teal lived at the Lumb, Millbank and later at Cote Hill, Burnley Road. Mrs Greenwood's aunt lived at Star Cottage, at the rear of the pub, in a house which had a dug-out toilet which was emptied periodically by the Sowerby Bridge Urban District Council. The Greenwoods left the Manse in 1975 but Colin remembers it as being a very happy, peaceful and a pleasant house to live in. He is well-known locally and has had a shop in Sowerby Bridge where he sells gifts, cards and jewellery since 1976. Earlier he was in business at 45, Bolton Brow, now Lee Brothers' Motorcycles. Here he started by selling antiques but when they became expensive he began to sell other items. Colin now lives at Prospect Avenue, Pye Nest.

The stage in the Congregational Chapel had heavy curtains hanging at the sides and unfortunately there was a large pillar in the centre of the stage which somewhat broke up the line of vision so there could be some aspiring actor hidden behind it when a performance was being given. Beyond were the kitchen and the primary room where the young pupils would have their lessons. I remember the sandpit with its animals and figures and pieces of mirror used to represent water. There would be stories about Jesus and his disciples, and classes usually taken by teachers Margaret Kerridge and Margaret Jowett, friends who served the chapel for many years and organised numerous special services and events. They wrote verses for us children to recite and perform on these occasions and also ran the Girl Guides and Brownie classes. I joined the Brownies hoping to be a "Fairy" but I had to be content with being a "Pixie". There was quite a wait for a uniform, so the only thing I had was my own brown beret. After a while I dropped out, I'm not sure why – perhaps I felt a bit silly with just the beret! Pat Dixon was in the Girl Guides at the chapel in the White Heather troupe, and every third Sunday they marched from St Peter's Church up through the village to the Old Green Chapel.

She enjoyed when it was her turn to carry a flag on the parade. They marched into the upstairs chapel and carried the flags down to the front before the service began. Carrying the flag too high on one occasion, it caught the roof under the balcony making an awful noise, but no damage to the brass top of the flagpole. Pat remembers the guides going on walks and picnics during the summer, making a campfire and cooking "fattie" cakes.

"Old Green" Annual Whitsuntide Walk with the Sunday School Banner,
off St Peter's Avenue, Beechwood, 1938.

The classes for the older pupils were situated off the main schoolroom downstairs and usually Lizzie Carter and Fenetta (Hettie) Haigh would teach the girls. They lived in cottages across from the Star Inn. Lizzie had a cleft palate so she spoke rather strangely and wore her hair in "earphone" plaits wound round and round over her ears. She was a lovely lady, and as children we would call and see her in her gas-lit home. I think Hettie lived next door with her sister Rose and brother George. At the rear of the stage was a passage to gain access upstairs, leading into an area with a toilet and vestry. Through a door you entered the upper chapel. This was a huge and impressive space with a pulpit up some steps and a roped-off area with communion table and chairs. High up was the organ with its silver pipes behind, the organist sitting with a brass rail and a short curtain to his back, the choir stalls in front and to each side. There was an upper balcony and through the windows views up to Well Head, with Arthur Maskill's cows grazing in the fields. Some of the downstairs pews, down the sides of the chapel, were box-style with little doors that fastened with a catch. The central ones also had door and had runners of burgundy-coloured carpet to sit on. Some worshippers always sat in the same pews.

"The Ballyhooligans" performed in "Country Capers", presented by The Old Green Revellers, at Sowerby Congregational Church, Saturday, March 6th, 1954. Left to right: Ronnie Holt, ?, Martin Bottomley, David Sutton, Trevor Whitworth. Rear, John Kerridge, Brian Wilson. Front left to right, Eric Moore, Barry Ackroyd, Raymond Barrett.

We would have Sunday school outings to the seaside and other destinations. They were eagerly anticipated and enjoyed by all who went on them. Plays would be performed and nativity plays at Christmas. It was great fun getting dressed up and making sure that we all knew the lines and words we had to say and come in at the right time. Once I was a playing a card "painting the roses red" in "Alice in Wonderland", another time the angel Gabriel in a nativity play. All this activity and participation was good for boosting confidence and learning lines of verse, always so much easier when young! We used to bring home missionary boxes to collect our spare pennies and persuade our friends and family to make donations. The money was then used abroad, possibly for missionaries working in Africa. There were autumn fairs and three-day "At Homes" were held at Christmas. There were stalls with lots of home-made produce to buy such as jams, marmalade and pickles, all made with fruit and vegetables grown in allotments and gardens. This event was handy for getting in a few Christmas gifts while supporting the chapel. There would be concerts with visiting performers, singers and people reciting poetry and telling tales. Jumble sales were held regularly and were very well attended. Tables would be full of assorted items of clothing, which would be carefully sorted through by purchasers looking for bargains. Other household bric-a-brac would be on sale and people would spend a few coppers and take home carrier bags stuffed with their bargains.

Sunday School outing – Southport, 1960 or 1961.

My mother would take me along to the Co-op in Sowerby Bridge, to select our outfits for the anniversary in good time as things got "picked through". We would enter the large premises through the ground floor full of girls' and boys' school uniforms, menswear and shoes. Upstairs passing the window where you could see the River Calder below, your feet now stood on a rubber mat connected to bell which announced your arrival. One year mother bought a coral pink bouclé wool coat with a neat "Peter Pan" collar. It was a stunner with its fitted style and flaring full skirt. To complete the outfit, she teamed the coat with a feathered half hat in shades of pink to deep coral, gunmetal grey shoes, handbag and grey nylon gloves. She looked very stylish but the outfit was rather impractical and a bit too posh for general wear. I used to take it out of her wardrobe, hold it against me and "pretend" that I was wearing it. When I was in my teens I was bought a summer light woollen coat in duck egg blue. It had a fairly large collar that stood up a little, several medium-sized buttons and a flaring skirt. The sleeves were three-quarter length so I wore a pair of long white gloves with ruching at the cuffs. The back had detail as there was a large inverted pleat in the swagger, kept in shape by a "V" of material that fastened onto two buttons, or you could remove it and let the back swing loosely. This again was not particularly practical but it was certainly stylish. Everyone made an effort to be smart and older ladies wore hats in all shapes and colours, selected to complement their outfits.

"Old Green" Sunday School Anniversary – 1955.
Back row, left to right, John Kerridge, Eric Moore, Audrey Moore, Margaret Kerridge,
Margaret Jowett.
Next to back row, L to R, Jean Smith (myself) Jean Brayshaw, Paulette Margetts, Joan
Bottomley, Margaret Hunt, Ann Lane, Lizzie Carter, Hettie Haigh, Geoffrey Greenwood,
Harry Greaves.
Third row from back, L to R, Dorothy Gill, Sandra Midgley, Ann Sugden, Trevor
Laycock, Rodney Rushworth, Ian Hitchen, Ronnie Holt.
Second row from front, L to R, Ruby Bottomley, Sylvia Walker, John Wilson, Barrie
Ackroyd, Brian Laycock, Trevor Crowther, Peter Rushworth, Malcolm Midgley.
Front row, L to R, ?, Phillip Irons, Sybil Bland, next three children, plus first ? brothers
& sisters, surname Holroyd, Geoffrey Laycock, Vera Midgley, ?, Joan Crowther,
Barbara Hitchen.
Perhaps someone can complete the missing names?

Mother did not like to wear a bra or a bust bodice as she sometimes called them. Thin straps annoyed her as they would always be slipping off her shoulders and her vests and petticoats always had to have "built up shoulders" to prevent this. As she had very little bosom it really didn't make much difference to her appearance, though I do remember at one time she had an unusual cotton bra which had a pocket in each cup where you could insert a plastic straw, blow into it and, like magic, increase your bust size and become curvaceous. This mysterious object was kept in a box on the upper shelf in her wardrobe and I used to take it out occasionally and study it as a child! I do not recall this magic bra ever being worn. My own personal problem began at senior school when it became clear during PE lessons that I needed to start wearing a bra. Most of my friends were wearing one by now but Mother did not understand my plight. So I took myself off to Sowerby Bridge to a shop called Toll's just over the bridge on the right-hand side of the road. For the sum of 3/11d I bought my first bra, which I probably had to launder myself! Starting being "grown up" and having my first period wasn't very enlightening either. Mother handed me a piece of flannelette sheeting and a couple of safety pins and that was how you coped. After all the passing years I remember distinctly what my mother said to me, "Welcome to the joys of being a woman", not very reassuring to a thirteen-year-old who was feeling somewhat apprehensive at the onset of the monthly cycle. After use the sheeting strips were put into a bucket of salted cold water to soak, washed out and then reused. This method of protection was not unusual when money was tight and the luxury of chemist-bought products was probably beyond the budget of many families. Later I discovered Lilia sanitary towels and the luxury of a sanitary belt: how times have changed! We had very little education on the facts of life at school, just a talk about periods from an embarrassed-looking teacher. Mother certainly didn't broach the subject and I never felt able to ask her anything. Most of the bits and pieces of information I knew were collected from the playground and school friends, not the best way of learning about an important part of one's future life.

At chapel, prizes for good attendance were usually presented to pupils at special services. Several of mine are tucked away in the attic but one that is now in use again to read to my grandson Hugo is the book "The Little Brown Bears at the Zoo" by Chris Temple. It was given to me in December 1950 and as a child I loved the short stories of the little bear's adventures, as Hugo does now. Another prize was called "Marigold in Godmother's House", another favourite. Sometimes a child received a Bible as a prize. When your name was called out, you had to go to the front to accept it from the person who had been chosen to present them. It felt good to take a book prize home and to know that it was yours to keep.

The Harvest Festival was a lovely time of year when the chapel would be decorated and filled with fruit, vegetables and flowers. Every window bottom had a vase or jug of flowers and greenery. I remember purple Michaelmas daisies and colourful dahlias, most of them grown in people's gardens or allotments. The tables at the front would be overflowing with home-grown produce, displayed around a wheatsheaf of home-baked bread. Leading up to the Harvest I would try to get hold of a strawberry basket, or an empty mushroom basket, from Bob Steadman, the greengrocer, to put my contribution of goodies in. If Bob had some packing straw to spare it was a bonus, as the fruit looked better sitting on top of that. The basket would then be covered with some coloured paper and the handle bound. Then I would carefully select my assortment of fruit and perhaps a nice brown hen's egg, put some scrunched up tissue paper in the bottom of the basket, then the straw and start to "arrange" the items, usually apples, oranges, bananas and a small bunch of grapes to top them off. Then a final covering of cellophane paper and my harvest basket was ready. At a point during the service, maybe after singing "We Plough the Fields and Scatter", the children would take their contributions to the front and these would be laid along the step that ran in front of the raised area, making a splendid display of fresh produce. Today many of the items given at harvest time are tinned goods which are easy to distribute and non-perishable, but they do not have the same attraction as all the fresh fruit and vegetables had. The items would be taken to people in the village who would be thankful to receive them. Two popular harvest hymns were "All Good Gifts Around Us" and "All Things Bright and Beautiful". The scholars would also participate with some sort of presentation. I remember one where the word "Harvest" was spelt out by the first child having a large letter "H" on a piece of card, saying their piece beginning with that letter, the next one with the letter "A" and so on until the full word was spelt out. It was probably written and thought up by the two Margarets who worked so hard writing and producing items for the children to perform at the chapel's celebrations and events.

Another chapel that organised activities, held concerts and social events was Rooley Lane Chapel, where Gordon Smith, Rita Spence and Ann Mairn ran a group of Scouts and Cubs.

Rooley Lane Chapel 40th Halifax Group Cubs and Scouts, about 1950.
Back row: Leaders, Gordon Smith, Rita Spence, Ann Mairn, John Clinton.
Middle row: David Hartley, Bobby Dennis, Geoffrey Wadsworth?, Ian Cowan, Terry Bottomley.
2nd to front row: John Charnley, Donald Bower.
Front row: John Easton, Roland Smith, Granville Bower, Colin Spence, Harry Nelson.

Sowerby Post Office

Sowerby Post Office in the 1940s – looking down Town Gate.

Just up the road from our house was the Post Office, a 17th-century building with a stone porch which had first opened as a Post Office in 1914. When I was a child it was run by Mr Harry Haigh and his wife Constance (Connie, was the daughter of Bob Holland the butcher). They had two children, Mary and Stuart. Previous postmasters were Jimmy Nicholl, Hanson Haigh who was Harry's uncle, and the Smethursts. Harry and Connie Haigh took over in May 1934 when Mary was six months old. My friend Margaret's parents, Mr Selwyn and Mrs Elizabeth (Betty) Hunt, took over from the Haighs in 1959 and a year later they moved down to the newly-built parade of shops and the new Post Office there, living in the flat above the premises. They ran the Post Office from 1959 to 1973 when it was taken over by the Corboy family. Mr Bill Corboy was thought by the GPO to be too old to be trained for the job, but he was able to help his daughter Sheila and son-in-law Bev who acted as the postmaster. They "inherited" Joan McDanielson as an assistant in the shop from the Hunts. Later Hazel Bradley worked part-time in the shop and the Post Office. Mr and Mrs Corboy retired during the '80s, Mr Corboy first, followed some time later by his wife. When Joan and Hazel retired, several assistants followed to work there and these were trained by the Post Office as computers were now in use. Many local Post Offices were to close and Sowerby was no exception, closing for business in February 2004, much to the consternation of local pensioners who had collected their pensions there for many years. People now faced a journey to the Beechwood Post Office counter inside the supermarket on Fore Lane

Avenue or a trip into Sowerby Bridge or to Halifax to collect their pensions. Petitions were signed and letters sent to the *Evening Courier* in support of local Post Offices but all to no avail, and several closed in our area. Sheila and Bev continued to run the grocery side of the business until the lease ran out in April 2006 and they retired. Brenda Sweeney has since taken over the new lease.

The porch of the old Post Office had a stone bench seat on the left-hand side and opposite it there was a glass case with doors that opened so that advertising posters could be displayed on the inside. The porch was a popular rendezvous for courting couples to use in the evenings and for the young people of the village to meet in. Perhaps because of the porch, it was rather dark inside the shop. Some goods, such as sacks of potatoes and bundles of firewood, were on display on the stone floor. The Post Office counter was inside to the left and the counter for groceries was in front of the living quarters to the rear. There was an assortment of sweets and goodies for children on the counter, liquorice sticks in jars, Spanish sticks, sherbet dabs and pastel-coloured sherbet in glass jars, aniseed balls and gobstoppers from large to huge in size! There were sticks of coltsfoot rock, love hearts with messages printed on them, favourites to pass onto someone you liked at school perhaps, bonbons and marzipan teacakes, torpedoes, dolly mixtures, cherry lips, Parma violets and Mattock's toffees made down the road in Sowerby Bridge. For the more mature sweet-eater there were Poor Bens, Victory Vs and Chlorydine Tablets and tiny black Imps, sold to help ease winter sore throats and coughs. In summer there was ice cream from the fridge.

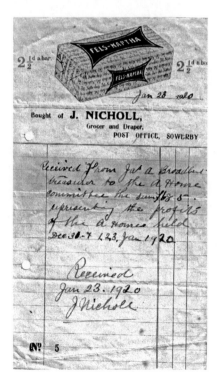

The rationing of food ended in 1954: I can remember seeing the rationing book with the coupons inside - Mother kept it in the roll top desk.

The grocery section also sold groceries, tinned items, sometimes apples, bread and confectionery from Broadbent's bakery at Shield Hall Lane. There was also a bread delivery from Whittle's in Lancashire. Fireworks were sold before Plot night, as well as cinder toffee and treacle toffee. Ben Ackroyd told me that Fenella Rawson would ride her donkey right into the shop when the Haighs were there. Pat Dixon also remembers that on occasions if Mr Haigh was short of coins, he would give you a stamp in lieu of change.

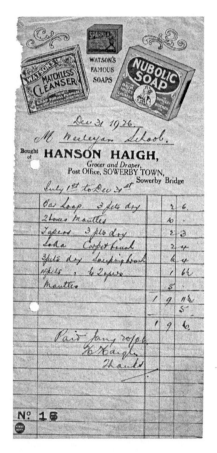

From my spending money each week (I cannot remember how much I was given) I would buy a Saving Stamp from the Post Office; it cost me six old pennies and the stamp had a picture of a young Princess Anne on. I would stick this into a special book and when it was full the stamps could be redeemed for cash. This money would most likely be used towards some item of clothing for me. The upper value stamp was out of my saving power at half a crown each (two shillings and six old pennies). Prince Charles's picture was on these.

The Post Office was quite a meeting-place for the various vicars in the village. They would congregate there to discuss certain topics of the day and matters that needed their attention – the Rev. RH Lazell, vicar at Steep Lane, the Rev. R Handyside from the Old Green chapel, the Rev. Gibson from St Peter's Church and Mr Haigh. The Haighs were very helpful people who contributed much to the village, their customers and to the people of Sowerby in general. The Post Office was a much-used facility in the village.

Harry Haigh wearing his official chain sees off a group of Sowerby pensioners on a day's outing in the mid-'50s.

Mr Haigh was also a member of Sowerby Bridge Council for twenty-one years. He was chairman from 1950 to 1951 and served on the West Riding Urban District Council's association for a number of years, representing the council on a number of outside authorities, which included the Calder Divisional Education Executive. He was also chairman of the Sowerby Bridge Primary School managers and a governor of Sowerby Bridge Grammar and Secondary Schools. With interests in the welfare of young and old alike, he was president of the Sowerby and Beechwood Old Age Pensioners' Association, chairman of the SBUDC Old Peoples' Welfare Committee, a keen church worker at Rooley Lane Methodist Church and steward of Sowerby Bridge Methodist Church. He was postmaster at Sowerby for twenty-five years before moving to live at Washington House at Hubberton.

The village's red telephone kiosk stood outside the post office; the next nearest one was at Pollit Avenue. The telephones were the black handset type with four old pennies needed to make a call. Press button A to be put through and press button B to get your pennies back!

Above the Post Office there was a building which was used as a smithy and I have vague memories of seeing large working horses being trimmed up with ribbons of red and blue in their manes, plaited straw and leather and brass harnessing. This was most probably for some annual ceremony that took place in the village, perhaps May Day. Above the smithy were numbers 57 to 59, Town Gate and next there was a large yard which had several buildings in it. My father used to keep his black taxis up here and hold occasional sales – once it was of fire-damaged stock that he had bought somewhere. Lynn Medlock, now living in Malaga, Spain, remembers items bought from a sale held in a large hut in the yard when she was a child. Lynn and her sister Pat, who lives in Canada, were beneficiaries when their mother Edna (née Morgan) bought them a pair of clogs and a waistcoat each from one of these sales, as well as crayons and colouring books. The Medlock family used to live at the top house in Haigh's Buildings.

Next door to them lived Mrs Briggs who would keep the bus drivers and conductors on the Hubberton and Steep Lane runs supplied with jugs of tea. They would nip off the bus to collect the jug and take it to whichever terminus they were en route to. Their tea break would be taken by the telephone kiosk at Steep Lane or opposite "The Riggin" at Hubberton. On the return journey the jug would be deposited back with Mrs Briggs. She must have brewed up countless jugs of tea over the years!

At the bottom house lived Mr Kenneth and Mrs Iris Lum with their daughter Kathleen. They later moved to Prospect House, Rooley Lane. At the back of Haigh's Farm, facing into the fields, lived Willie Lang and his wife. He was well known as a cornet player and member of Back Dyke Mills Band. Lynn and her family used to listen to him practising his pieces. Mother used to tell me that he could play "The Post-horn Gallop" and was excellent on the post-horn. Later in that house lived Mr Ernest and Mrs Freda Whiteley (Jean Brayshaw's sister). The local window-cleaner had a shock of hair which earned him the nickname "Fuzzy Wuzzy" from the children but it wasn't meant in a disrespectful way. I can also remember Mr and Mrs Conway living at Haigh's Buildings with their little son Barrie who sadly died at a young age. Behind the Post Office were the allotments where Percy Stott of St Peters Avenue used to grow an assortment of flowers and vegetables. Memories come back here of going to see him with money clutched in my hand to purchase some of the Sweet Williams that he had grown.

Mrs Iris Lum was a key figure in the village as for many years she organised coach trips for the locals. Yarmouth and Bridlington were favourite destinations visited for a week's holiday and these ran for several years. My mother and I went to Bridlington for a few years and enjoyed boat trips on the "Yorkshire Belle". There were also trips to the illuminations at Blackpool and Morecambe, and usually a stop on the way home for some good old Yorkshire fish and chips to enjoy out of the wrapper

Mrs Iris Lum and her accordion.

Pantomimes around the Christmas period were popular and I remember going to see Ken Platt of "I won't take my coat off, I'm not stopping" fame. Another outing was to see "Rose Marie on Ice", a spectacular show and the Mounties in their red uniforms looked very smart. I can remember the excitement of going to visit the Edinburgh Tattoo because it was held at night-time and the arena was floodlit. We had a travelling rug wrapped around our knees to keep cosy in the night chill. These trips and excursions were wonderful adventures for me as a young girl and Mrs Lum without doubt brought a great deal of happiness to the children and adults of Sowerby village. She also provided the entertainment for the coach party by playing her piano accordion on the return journey. There would follow a session of popular songs and tunes of that era. The ones that always got us all singing along were "The Happy Wanderer (Valderie)", "A Windmill in Old Amsterdam", "On Ilkla Moor Bah' Tat", "Ten Green Bottles" and "One Man Went to Mow", this usually ending up at a very fast pace and with everyone laughing. The only problem was that when Iris played she would start at the front of the coach and song by song work her way up the aisle to the back, stay a while, then return to the front again. If she decided to lean against your seat and play her accordion it was rather loud, but she just smiled and played on, the instrument strapped across her ample bosom. What a pity these performances were never captured on film to show the real essence of the '50s and how people enjoyed these outings.

When Mr and Mrs Dixon, Pat and Terry with aunties Clarice and Florrie went on holiday to relatives in Newton-upon-Rawcliffe near Pickering, they would be taken by my father in one of his big black taxis. My brother David went along with them for the ride. After their stay Dad would return to transport the family back to Sowerby in style.

Local families on the harbour at Bridlington, 1953, ready to begin a week's holiday, organised by Iris Lum.

Mum and I in Blackpool, May 1954. Note the "formal dress" – even the dreaded bowler hat went with us.

The other side of the counter at the Co-op

I spoke to Pat Dixon because she knew I was very interested in her time working at Sowerby Co-op. When I went to talk to her at her home at Willow Gardens in July 2005, she handed me nineteen pages of her memories written on a notepad. They are most interesting and as far as possible I shall interpret them as she presented them herself.

Pat was born in January 1941 and left Sowerby New Road Girls' School when she was fifteen years old. She started work at the Co-op and paid all her wages to her mother until she was twenty-one years old; only then did she pay board money. The Co-op was situated in Town Gate where Harry's Supermarket is now. Mr Barnes was the boss and Edgar Judson and Reggie Whitworth also worked there.

All the staff wore white overalls with long sleeves and the girls also wore a white apron over the overall which was changed every day. On Mondays some of the girls did the weighing and the bagging of the rice and dried peas which came in brown hessian sacks and were measured out into one-pound blue paper bags. The currants and sultanas were in wooden boxes and were also bagged into the blue bags. Sometimes when these had been stored for a long time there would be grubs among them. Lard was in a large block inside a cardboard box; it was cut to size and then wrapped in greaseproof paper. Coffee came in a large drum and was weighed out into four-ounce greaseproof bags; by the time the whole drum had been done, the girls would be feeling sick with the smell. Nothing was prepared as it is today and all the stock came from the warehouse in Sowerby Bridge. When the lorry arrived at the front door everyone had to help to unload it by hand. There were beautiful scales in the store, some made of brass, for weighing anything from fish to sweets. The cheese-cutter was white marble and two electric machines were used for slicing bacon and a smaller hand one for ham and cooked meats. The Co-op had its own brand of margarine; Red label was the cheapest, Silver the mid-priced brand and Gold label the most expensive. The boxes of soap and soap powder contained a sheet of stamps for customers to collect with a free gift as an eventual incentive. The bread was uncut, small and large loaves and teacakes, to be put into white paper bags for the journey home. Most of the shops had a grocery, fruit and vegetable section as well as fish, confectionery and a butcher's department. Sowerby had a small butcher's shop up the road in Town Gate, with Geoffrey Gledhill working there for a long time until the house next door to Sowerby Co-op was put up for sale and the butchery section then moved into those premises.

There were shelving and differing-sized drawers all around the shop. The muslins which the cheeses were wrapped in were used afterwards for cleaning cloths and dishcloths. Some customers would leave their grocery order to be made up by the staff and delivered by the store's lorry driver. Over the course of a day's work, the assistants would walk miles around the shop. They would put every item onto the counter, adding it up in their heads as they went round because nothing had a price label on. Each assistant had a place around the counter with a drawer for the takings and a pad to write down the customers' Co-op dividend numbers and how much they had spent. After a while the "divi" numbers were remembered automatically, ours was 675 and the

Dixons' divi numbe was 8055. The coins were farthings, halfpennies, threepenny bits, sixpence, two shillings, half-a-crowns, ten-shilling notes, one-pound notes, and the large white five-pound notes. When Pat began to work for the Co-op, she was shown how to spot the counterfeit white fivers, as they were called. As a junior assistant Pat used to put the shop's takings from the tills in two brown paper bags and walk all the way to the Co-op offices in West End, deposit them there and walk all the way back to Sowerby again. It was a very happy time and the staff had lots of fun, sometimes larking about unloading the lorries but nobody was cross when this happened. The sacks containing the yellow or white stones used for edging doorsteps had to be handled carefully or there would be dust all over the aprons and overalls, which would then have to be changed. Sometimes if another branch needed helping out due to holidays or sickness, staff from the Sowerby store were asked to help out for a period of time. The shop stayed open on Friday nights until 7pm, Wednesday was half day and on Saturdays it closed at 1pm.

Pat worked at Sowerby Co-op for two and a half years, leaving to go and train as a burler and mender at Longbottom's Mill in Sowerby Bridge, where she worked for many years.

Providence Chapel

Providence Chapel prior to demolition in the early 1960s.

Pat's memories:

Providence Methodist Chapel stood in the middle of Sowerby village, set back off the road. It was a large building with gardens on either side of a long pathway and a separate toilet block outside. My Auntie Florrie was caretaker at the chapel and her sister Clarice and brother Stanley (my dad) helped to run the building. My father's main job was to attend to the boiler house, shovelling the coke into the cellar after a delivery. It was especially important to keep the fire going in winter. We would all help with the cleaning, scrubbing the floors, polishing the numerous windows and the never-ending dusting. We did all the catering for funerals and weddings, putting out large tables in the big room and covering them with the lovely white tablecloths which Auntie Florrie sent to the laundry. The chapel's white and blue crockery was brought out, and the large tea urns.

Chapel anniversaries were a big event and involved hours of preparation. Jellies were made in every colour and there were dishes of salad with boiled eggs and cooked meats. Cakes and bread were bought at the Co-op and I would fill a big table with glass fruit dishes and put in jelly, fruit custard and cream. There was lots of help from Mrs Speak of Beechwood, who would slice and butter all the bread and from another helper, Mrs White of Hubberton, who washed all the lettuces and made up the plates of salad. When all the food was prepared and ready, it had to be carried on full trays up into the Sunday school room from the cellar below. One of the hardest parts for dad was having to carry the large tea urns up from the cellar containing boiling water, and later big white jugs of steaming hot water. Then, when the celebration was over and people were getting ready for the evening service, we had to take everything back down to the cellar and tackle all that washing up – if only dishwashers had been invented then!

There was certainly plenty to do, what with jumble sales, Shrove Tuesday events and autumn fayres. We had to help dad weed the paths around the chapel and wash them down with caustic soda and keep the gardens neat and tidy. For Communion services, Auntie Florrie would cut the bread into tiny pieces and fill the small glasses with wine. Before she was caretaker at Providence, Auntie Florrie did a similar job at Rooley Lane Chapel. Choosing the right outfit for chapel anniversaries could take months – if you were a little better off, you might in fact have more than one outfit, or at least a different hat for different occasions! Rather like a fashion show, it was the "highlight" of the year.

Sowerby Tennis and Bowling Club – early 1920s.

Another centre of village social life was **Sowerby Tennis and Bowling Club**. Mrs Mary Dale told me about this aspect of Sowerby life. Born Cicely Mary Taylor in Leeds in 1915, she moved to Dewsbury in 1930 and then at the age of 20 she moved to Sowerby Bridge. She thought that the town was the last place that God had made and still does! Mrs Dale, her late husband Jack and their daughter Elizabeth lived in St Peter's Avenue. While worshipping at Bolton Brow Chapel, Mary met a lady tennis player who introduced her to Sowerby Tennis and Bowling Club. Situated down Back Lane just below the church and the allotments (now Church Close), the club held numerous social events and seemed at the time to be the hub of the village. Plays were produced by Fred Hartley, and Mary remembers performing in an entertainment called "Pink String and Ceiling Wax". On two occasions a May Queen pageant was held, when young men were good sports and dressed up in ladies' attire to be attendants to the "Queen", played by a man! Other attendants included a mayor, mayoress, mace bearer, judge, and a crown bearer.

May Queen Pageant, Sowerby Tennis & Bowling Club.
Rear, left to right, Harry Haigh (Mayor), Grace Longbottom (Mayoress)
Verny Mitchell (Soldier).
Front, Kenneth Taylor (Attendant,) Desmond Howe (Seated, Queen)
Leslie Harkness (Attendant. End Right, Willie Ackroyd
Rodney Stafford (Boy Crown Bearer).

During winter months the old men who were club members played card games in the pavilion while Mary and her friends enjoyed a game of table tennis or darts. Members were eager to be allowed to play tennis on Sundays but the members who attended church and chapel were against this. A meeting was held, chaired by Arthur Binns, and all the club members who attended decided that Sunday tennis should go ahead. Mary used the word "clamouring" to describe how the players wanted the Sunday tennis to be voted for. Not having heard this word used for a very long time, we looked it up in her dictionary and found the word "eager" is now the one most likely to be used. But the decision was not popular with all members and resulted in some of the older ones leaving the club as they were opposed to the very idea of sport on Sundays. This was probably some time during the 1950s but after a period of time people gradually returned to the club and soon harmony was restored among the members. When playing tennis, Mary wore a skirt but later when shorts came into fashion, she was the first lady at the club to wear them. Soon after other lady members followed her style and changed from skirts into shorts. Mary Ackroyd was another long time member of the club and she would walk down Town Gate in her tennis gear, racket in hand from her home at Green Cottage at the bottom of Rooley Lane, heading for an afternoon or evening of playing tennis.

Mary Dale enjoyed playing tennis and often was on the Sowerby team playing in local competitions. She carried on playing until the age of 70, when her daughter Elizabeth suggested that perhaps she was now too old to continue. So Mary switched to bowls and continued to play until a knee operation and failing eyesight brought her sport to a standstill and she then became a spectator. She joined the club in 1936 and has been involved in sporting life for more than 70 years. Another of her interests was singing and she joined the Sowerby Bridge Gilbert and Sullivan Society from 1940 until 1960, performing in concerts at Bolton Brow Chapel and later at Ryburn Secondary School, Sowerby. Mary remembers with fondness the happy times spent in Sowerby and we both enjoyed recalling her memories and looking through her collection of interesting photographs.

Field House, Dean Lane

Field-House. Triangle. Nr Halifax.

Along Dean Lane past Long Field, where Austin Mitchell, the MP for Grimsby, writer and broadcaster, now lives (his mother had lived there earlier), stands the imposing Field House, once the home of the Stansfeld family. The tall stone gateposts opposite, heading the carriage drive leading to the lodge at Triangle, no longer stand and the general state of the walling is poor due to neglect and theft of top stones. The Old Hall was built in 1630 by the rich Stansfeld family, and then in 1749 George Stansfeld built on the classic-style Georgian hall. The last direct descendant of this family, Mrs Mabel Stansfeld, died in July 1987 at the age of 96. The house contents were auctioned and raised £514,000. The Stansfelds were an important family in Sowerby and, like the Rawsons, owned land and property in the area. There used to be twenty farms on the estate and the warehouses at the rear of the building were used to store the cloth pieces woven by yeoman farmers on the surrounding hillsides. They would then be taken to the Piece Hall in Halifax and sold. The ancestry of the Stansfeld family could be traced back to Richard the Lionheart and at Field House they lived in grand style and employed staff to cater for their needs. Like the Rawsons, the Stansfelds attended St Peter's Church and provided some of the bells for the church. When the old Sowerby church was demolished during the eighteenth century and replaced by the present building, George Stansfeld removed windows and features from the building and used them at Field House. The bell tower and a Gothic-style window have been incorporated to the rear of the converted buildings and make an attractive feature.

Sir Ernest Hall, the millionaire entrepreneur who bought, rescued and built up the Dean Clough Mills empire in Halifax in 1971, became the second owner of the Field House estate when he bought it in the mid-1980s. He went to view a piano that was for sale and ended up buying the house, the estate which included fifty acres of parkland and fields, a farm, cottages and a boating lake. Extensive work then began on a restoration programme to provide accommodation in a sympathetic, fitting manner. The conversion of outbuildings into homes has created a new community on the former estate. Sir Ernest's son Jonathan lived there for some time, but the large house has now been divided into two dwellings so Field House continues to change with time.

The Field House estate was the venue for annual garden parties when I was a young girl. The Stansfelds opened the grounds, which would be filled with local families. There was a bran tub filled with sawdust and I remember shoving my hand deep inside hoping to get a good prize. There were stalls and attractions, and the boating lake was opened up for the day to provide boat rides. Somewhere in my memory there is the sight of a large parrot, with colourful red and blue feathers, its claws gripping onto a wooden perch.

Alice In Wonderland Dancers at Field House 1951.
Front left, Dawn Holt; front right, Jacqueline Haines.
Left to right rear: ?; Susan Feather as Alice, ?, Shirley Mitchell, Angela Robinson as Bunny, ?
Front Centre, Susan Turner. Behind, Malan Ford.

The big attraction was the dancing display, given on the wooden stage erected in the grounds. The dancers were all pupils of Miss Marion Hitchen's School of Dance in Sowerby Bridge. When I was about nine years old and a pupil there, I also got my chance to dance at Field House. I can remember being a member of the chorus for "I

Love the Sunshine of your Smile" and "You Should See Me Dance the Polka". The night before the dancing display I would have my hair put up in rags by my mother to create ringlets for the show – they were rather uncomfortable to sleep in! Malan Ford and Angela Robinson, who both had private lessons with Miss Marion, used to perform solo and take the lead in performances. In one dance display, "Alice in Wonderland", Angela wore a white knitted bunny outfit, complete with ears and fluffy tail. Another routine I remember Angela dancing was "The Sailor with the Navy-Blue Eyes". My tap shoes only had the taps on the toes and I wished that I had some on my heels too, like some of the other pupils! The lino upstairs at home in Town Gate used to get some practising done on it, until mother heard me and would shout upstairs and tell me to stop. Once, arriving at Field House to dance, I realised that I only had one ballet shoe with me so Maureen Creamer went all the way back to my home to pick up the one I had left behind.

Malan Ford tying her ballet shoes. (Note the wind-up gramophone, also on the stage a sand filled fire bucket as a safety regulation.)

Names I remember from dancing class were Angela Robinson, Kathleen Coggin, Dawn Holt, Shirley Mitchell, Brenda Swatridge, Margaret Barraclough and the late Jacqueline Haines. We all used to attend senior school together at Sowerby New Road

School and many of these girls have remained lifelong friends. Marion Hitchen (Elwin) was born in 1931 at New Drop, Broad Lane, Sowerby, and she used to perform in pantomimes at Sowerby Tennis Club and at local chapels. She also performed on stage at the Palace Theatre in Wards End, Halifax, right up to the last show, "The King and I", before the building was demolished in August 1959. When Marion was fourteen years she had taught at Madame Ibbotson's in Prescott Street, Halifax, and then when she was eighteen, she responded to a request from the girls in Sowerby to find some premises and start up a dancing school. Classes were held in several locations in Sowerby Bridge, firstly at Owencho Chambers, Wharf Street, where two rooms were made into one large one for lessons. Then the classes moved to Grange House, formerly the Crown public house, behind the Christadelphian Hall in Wharf Street. Later there was a move to Hollins Mill Lane, and again to a room opposite the Library. The final move was to rooms above Vera Ingham's Jubilee Café at the bottom of the old Tuel Lane. Marion ended her dancing classes in 1963. Without doubt her dedication to performing and teaching dancing provided much entertainment over the years for the local community. Besides raising her own family, Marion became a figurehead for many of her pupils and has been, and still is, held in high esteem and respect. Also connected with dancing displays in the Sowerby area were Harry and Marion Lumb of King Street. Mr Lumb played the piano at shows and garden parties and his wife was a helper.

Robinson Crusoe Pantomime, St Peter's School, 1949 (Sowerby Pantomime Society).
Left to right rear, Lloyd Bohan, Delia Kellett, Terry Coley, Joyce Thompson,
Malan Ford, Joyce Jackson (Robinson Crusoe – Principal Boy) and Dorothy Nutton
(Polly Perkins, Principal Girl).
Front: Jim Wilson?, Willie Ackroyd, Desmond Howe.

Dancers in Robinson Crusoe Pantomime, 1949.
Back, left to right: Delia Kellett, Mavis Clarke, Bronwyn Crowther, Betty Ollerenshaw, Joyce Jackson (at rear), Doris Marlor, June Hartley, Pauline Gothard. Front, left to right: Mary Horner, Doreen Wadsworth, Muriel Wilson, Margaret Bower, Agnes Ward, Phyllis Beaumont, June Clarke. Front: Malan Ford.

The Conservative Club, Town Gate, Sowerby

Church Stile Farm
Pinfold Lane
Barn
Town Farm
34, 36 Highfield Place
New house built on what was Jack Wilcock's hen pen

Sowerby New Rd
Queen St
Park
King St
(What was) Conservative Club
32, Town Gate Where I was born
Town Gate
Council Flats

Aerial view c. 1988.

Before the building was divided into three dwellings, this large block was a Conservative Club. The caretakers here at one time were Edgar and Annie (née Kerridge) Helliwell: they had children, Donald, Kenneth, Randal, Blanche, Hazel and Mildred. Blanche was born at No. 32, on January 14, 1922. The address was then 32, Conservative Club House. Adele Kerridge who lived across the road at 36, Highfield Place was her aunt. Blanche is half cousin to the Kerridges who lived in Queen Street. She lived at the club when it was divided into three houses. Milton and Ivy Smith were the first people to move into the middle section called Club House. Mr and Mrs Thomas Riley lived at No. 30, prior to the Barretts. Their children were called Albina, Eveline, Bessie, Annice, Eleanor, Bramwell and Donald.

Before the alterations took place, the building had a through passage from No. 30 to No. 32 from one end of the building to the other. The three steps to the door at No. 30 were most likely to be one of the entrances to the club: at one time a mounting block was there. The doorstep at No. 32 is also of interest with its unusual half moon design, which is well worn at each side, and may have been used as another entrance to the club. There was a billiards room that ran the extent of the upper floor. Blanche recalls that most of the men in the village were away serving in the war, so the club was not used then to its full extent.

Clockwise from top - Sylvia Lodge, Terry Dixon, me and Shep about 1948; sisters Blanche and Hazel Helliwell; me, Terry Dixon and Tiny, approx. 1947; Blanche and her brother Randal Helliwell, late 1920s; Susan Greenwood, James and me, September 1971; Susan Greenwood and James, September 1971; me and Tiger, 1955.

Blanche's parents were the first caretakers of Sowerby Tennis & Bowling Club: the beautiful gardens there were tended by a gardener from Boulderclough. Her grandfather lived with Adele across at Highfield Place. He often went rabbit shooting, but later would only consume the brains from the creature's head! The Helliwell family used the washhouse in the yard across at Highfield Place, as the one in the back yard for No. 32 was still used as a slaughterhouse at that time; it also housed a stove to burn the animal waste.

For a short period of time the family moved into a small cottage down Littlewood Lane. There were two or three semi-dilapidated cottages there. Blanche's father was a farm labourer and had been asked by Joe Lumb who owned Row End Farm to look after some cattle for him. He also needed a tenant for the cottage, so the family moved in but only stayed for about nine months; the property was very basic and in a poor state of repair. They left here about 1930/31, moving back up to 28, Town Gate. When Blanche married her husband Edgar, the couple moved up to Spring Cottages in Hubberton to live. Their home is now in Skircoat Green Road, Halifax.

The Maskills at Well Head Farm

Muriel Maskill, a talented writer, poet and speaker, provided me with many interesting details about farming life at Well Head Farm in Sowerby where she lived with her late husband Arthur.

George Arthur Maskill was born in April 1929 at Haigh Top Farm in Barkisland, his grandfather Ben moving to the area from the family farm at Rodley in Leeds. Arthur's father James had followed him to Barkisland and Arthur was born soon after. When he was two years old, the family went to live at Broad Ings Farm at Rishworth and later they moved into Triangle where Arthur attended the local school when he was eight years old.

In 1942 his father took over the tenancy from the Rawson family of Well Head Farm, Sowerby. There was a problem with the former tenant (Edgar Barrett) and a year passed before they were able to move into the farmhouse. Arthur had some stock up at the farm and used to walk up from Triangle to Well Head to attend to the animals, later moving up to Sowerby at the age of fourteen. The farm had only fourteen acres of land so Arthur's father also took a job with the Post Office, working as Crown postman which gave him time to start farming in a small way at Well Head. With his pony and cart he also delivered coke from the gas house in Sowerby Bridge, furniture for Alec Smith, the joiner and cabinet maker in Town Gate, and bread in Sowerby and Boulderclough for Mr Lumb of Myrr Hill Bakery. Arthur also kept poultry and used to buy and sell pigs. He became friendly with my father, also called Arthur, who kept cattle at Stones Farm on Dob Lane, and also had the local butcher's shop in Town Gate. Arthur's pigs were killed at my dad's small slaughterhouse at Rooley Lane and the two men struck up a friendship which was extended to the two families. Food at this time was still rationed and Arthur Maskill's mother would make stand pies for my dad from the pork which he supplied. Even though there were restrictions in force to prevent it, the black market was in evidence and the two Arthurs had connections in Lancashire, transporting meat over the border, often during the night. Later Arthur Maskill obtained a licence through his father to produce milk at the farm and a mistal for only four cows was made in 1945.

Arthur's future wife, Muriel Broadhead, was born at Green Royd, Mount Tabor, in November 1928 by the light of candles and paraffin lamps. It was a very cold winter and a thin layer of ice covered the water that she was bathed in. The family moved to Pellon, where both sets of grandparents lived, when she was five years old. Her paternal grandfather, a Drum Major in the Duke's Territorial Army, was chief postman and in charge of the Telegraph boys at Halifax GPO. He also worked as a part-time sports reporter at the *Halifax Courier*. Muriel's maternal grandfather was a manager at WF Avery's Scales in King Cross Lane, Halifax.

Arthur and Muriel met in February 1948 at a dance at Thrum Hall Cricket Pavilion and their first date followed at a Young Farmers' Dance held on St Valentine's Day. When they were courting and, as they did not have a telephone at home, Arthur would ride his horse down to Sowerby Post Office to speak to Muriel from the telephone box there, his horse tethered nearby while he spoke to her. During their courting days and later when they were engaged, the couple used my father's taxi to pick up Muriel and take her to dances at the Queen's Hall on Queen's Road and at the Alexandra Hall in Halifax, and later home again. In 1948 Arthur's father decided to come out of Well Head Farm and concentrate on the saddlery business he had started in New Bank, Halifax, using skills he had learned during his time in the 1914-18 war. Arthur approached Fenella Rawson's grandmother (who was in charge at that time) about the tenancy of the farm for himself and this was granted. The story goes that she wrote down on an envelope, "Young Maskill takes over at Well Head". He was just nineteen years old at the time.

Arthur and Muriel were married at Christ Church, Pellon, in May 1950, and as Muriel did not want to live with her in-laws, the couple decided to set up home in a rented Rawson cottage in Rooley Lane. This was very basic one-up, one-down accommodation with a privy midden toilet, no tub, just a slab, emptied by the council muck cart! With three cottages sharing, a visit to the toilet must have been most unpleasant! Helen, the couple's first child, was born here in 1953, Hilary, their second daughter, was born at Well Head in 1955 and Stephen in 1959. They moved out of the cottage in 1952 when they exchanged with Arthur's parents at the farm. The rent was 3/- (15p) per week, including rates! Muriel worked as cashier at August's Engineers in King Cross. She was well educated and had secretarial skills, which included a shorthand speed of 100 words per minute. Earning a high salary, they were able to get the farm off to a good start by ploughing her wage back into the land and stock and also to take advantage of a Small Farmers' Scheme that was available then.

The farmhouse was basic and the water supply had to be pumped from a well down in the cellar, fed from another well in the field. The washing was done in the cellars with dolly-tub and wringer. More land was required for the farm so when Sowerby Bridge Urban District Council took over three of the Rawson family's fields in Rooley Lane for their building programme, Arthur was able to rent them. During the 1950s haymaking was done in these fields and Muriel remembers the horses pulling the machinery with hand labour to do the shaking, turning, ricking and piking of the hay. Arthur was the first farmer to own a hay-baler and he did contract baling in the summer while Muriel would do the milking in the parlour. The housing estate was built later and also the underground reservoir on these fields. The local cattle remover was Marshall Heap, and before Muriel and Arthur were married, Arthur would help him with his work to earn extra money. Mr Heap became ill and the business was sold to Edwin Robison, Arthur and Muriel's best man. Arthur helped Edwin to start up his business, Robison Brothers at Triangle. Muriel used to go in the cattle wagon with them to Arncliffe in Littondale, moving cattle from the Sowerby area to graze there for the summer. Sheep were then brought back to graze on land back at Sowerby for the winter. This proved to be a profitable enterprise and my father became involved with them. He also taught the lady farmer who took the cattle to drive a van and a tractor when horses became redundant.

Milking at the farm increased and during the early '60s the Maskills were the first farmers in the area to have cow cubicles and loose housing to replace the mistals. The Ministry of Agriculture, as it was known then, paid the farm many visits and representatives from Scotland came to see the new cubicle system. Later a milking parlour was built to milk two cows in tandem. It was an early example of automation and Muriel learned to operate the machinery, pulling levers to open the doors for the cows to come in from a collecting yard and into the parlour. She stood at a lower level to operate the milking machine and the milk then went straight into churns. A dairy was built and a bottling plant was installed in the old mistal. This was the beginning of semi-retail milk: now instead of the milk being sent to the Sowerby Bridge dairies run by Arthur Crossfield, it was bought by three dairy men to deliver in the Sowerby Bridge area – Philip Busfield who farmed at Triangle, Leonard Clay, a farmer at Brockwell (now a private housing estate) and Max Cockroft, whose father was a builder at Boulderclough. They picked milk up from Well Head Farm seven days a week. After rationing ended there were strict rules and regulations in operation and Mr Foster, Sanitary Inspector for Sowerby Bridge Urban District Council, would make regular visits to the farm to test the milk and inspect the premises. Farmers were penalised if there was not enough butterfat content – very different from today's dietary recommendations to drink skimmed and semi-skimmed milk.

During the '60s and the '70s, the Maskills rented Upper Quickstavers Farm, Upper Snape Farm and Old Barton and they later bought Lower Crow Hill Farm with twenty-four acres of land. They also acquired Ball Green Farm from Abraham Riley who had given up his tenancy to the Rawsons. Next was the tenancy of Joe Taylor's farm, Fields Farm at Mirey Lane. Muriel's daughter Helen has lived there since her marriage in 1974, later buying the house in the mid '90s when the Rawson estate was split after the death of Freddie Rawson's son (Fenella's brother). They were also offered Well Head, Ball Green and Fields Farm, land and buildings, which they bought as sitting tenants. The Maskills decided to take "the golden handshake" from the government in 1977 and after twenty-five years of producing milk, they went into rearing beef and sheep. Arthur's health had been suffering from allergies, which were related to the cattle and dust. He began to travel and to deal in cattle, visiting the northern markets and buying and selling animals to and from local farmers in Hebden Bridge, the Calder Valley and the Ryburn Valley.

During 1977 Muriel became involved with White Windows Cheshire Home at Sowerby. The support committee of Sowerby Bridge, of which Muriel was a member, held three dances in the sheep shed. The bar was run by Peter Meadowcroft of the Shepherd's Rest (Riggin) at Hubberton and music was provided by Shaun Gilligan's band from Oxenhope. Included in the ticket price of £2-50 was a homemade meat pie supper and a sweet to follow and there were competitions and a welly-throwing bout! All the profits from these events went to the home and between £200 and £300 was regularly raised. Barn dances were also held to raise cash for Sowerby Bridge Grammar School (Sowerby Bridge High School) where the Maskill children were pupils. Funds raised were used to pay for school equipment not paid for by West Riding County Council.

For Muriel and her friends, life in the village centred on the churches and chapels, on coffee mornings and afternoon teas. Mrs Stansfeld from Field House, Dean Lane, and Mrs Pease of The Breck, at Triangle, supported these, bringing produce from their gardens to sell. Arthur supplied the milk in a churn when annual bazaars were held in the Sunday school. Eighty pounds of piccalilli were made at the farm along with scones for the cake stall and afternoon teas. Field House was opened up and The Mother's Union at St Peter's Church, of which Muriel was a member, helped to organise refreshments and held competitions. In the 1970s Meals on Wheels began to operate in Sowerby and Beechwood areas. Marion Laycock, a stalwart worker at Old Green Chapel, and Muriel used to deliver the meals together to the elderly. Bed and breakfast was also run at Well Head Farm for a ten-year period by Muriel. The Traveller's Rest at Steep Lane had disco evenings and the Maskill girls enjoyed going there on Wednesday nights.

Both daughters went on to having successful careers, with Helen working as a journalist for some years at the *Evening Courier*. Hilary and her family now live in Canada, and Stephen has a butcher's shop in Hebden Bridge, and with his family lives at Well Head Farm. When Arthur and Muriel retired to Mytholmroyd, they both continued to be involved with the farm and business. Later Arthur became ill and had to spend time in hospital before coming home to be nursed and cared for by Muriel. Arthur's funeral was held at St Peter's Church on February 21 2006. The fitting quote on the funeral service card from Shakespeare's *Hamlet* read: "Let me be no assistant for a state, But keep a farm ......"

Arthur Maskill with his pups.

My writing has recorded some social history about Sowerby during my childhood. It is dedicated to all the people who know or have known Sowerby and hold it in their hearts.

Since completing my writing ------ Mrs Dale died on September 26, 2007 four days before her 92 birthday.

Stanley Mount died on October 14 2007, aged 83.

Ben Ackroyd now resides in a Residential Home in Savile Park.

Wood Lane Hall, described as a Grade 1 Listed Tudor Open Hall House was on the market with Ryburne & Co. of Hebden Bridge with a guide price of £1,300,000 on February 19th 2007.

"Middle Sowerby Hall", Town Gate, Sowerby and the adjoining cottage, were put up for auction by Brearley Greens during September 2007. It had been sold by early March 2008.

The three houses in Rooley Lane are now occupied.

The portrait of John Almighty was shown on the *Antiques Road Show* broadcast from Arundel Castle in West Sussex on September 9, 2007. Owned by a couple, the painting was valued at £2,500. How the portrait ended up there remains a mystery!

The vandalised East window at St Peter's Church has been repaired by specialists who worked on the restoration of York Minster. It was in place for the service held on Palm Sunday, 16th March 2008.

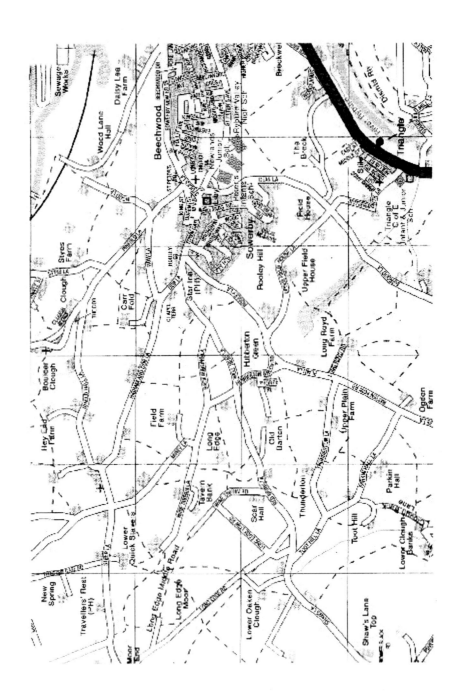

Lightning Source UK Ltd
Milton Keynes UK
03 April 2010

152292UK00001B/28/P